A Cry For I The Night

David Owen Ferrier

Battle Press
SATELLITE BEACH, FLORIDA

A Cry For Mercy In The Night

Battle Press books may be ordered through booksellers or by contacting:

Battle Press
1588 Highway A1A #B
Satellite Beach, FL 32937
1-919-218-4039
www.battlepress.media

ISBN: 978-1-5136-6803-1 (softcover)

Library of Congress Control Number: 2020919715.

Second Edition

"Those who danced were thought to be quite insane by those who could not hear the music."

Angela Monet (attributed)

And so it is with soldiers. I believe those of us who served hear a different song, dance still to the martial drum, and look not a little crazy to those who cannot hear our music.

Author's Note

This new edition is the product of a host of factors. Mainly I have been able to reduce print costs and subsequently the cover price of this edition. A good thing.

I have resisted the impulse to tinker with the contents though I have changed the order of several pieces, captioned the photos and added several new illustrations. Another good thing.

"Cry For Mercy" remains my most intimate, close to the heart rendering of my entire Vietnam experience leavened and enhanced by the comments and memories of my Dustoff family. Thank you for taking the time to read my book. I hope it helps in some way to increase your understanding of the hardships and sacrifices ALL veterans make.

Dedicated To:

The men, wives and families of the
571st medical detachment.

Lest We Forget.

INDEX

ACKNOWLEDGEMENTS 8
PREFACE 10
1967 12
D.E.A.D 14
B.C.T. 16
GETTING THERE 23
IN COUNTRY 26
FIVE ZERO SIX 29
FLYBOYS 30
CHERRY BOYS 32
THE GOOD GUYS 34
IS THAT GUY DEAD? 37
GOOKS 39
NAM STUFF 40
1968 42
1968 43
ANYTIME, ANYPLACE 44
HUE IN FLAMES 46
INCOMING 48
HOT L.Z's 49
CASUALTIES 51
FOX MIKE RADIO, MIDNIGHT SHIFT 53
KIA 56
BETTER HIM THAN ME 58
WRITING HOME 59
DON'T MEAN NOTHIN' 60
MORE NAM STUFF 61
HONOR WITHOUT MEDALS 62
NINETY ONE BRAVO 64
WHITE SHIPS NEARBY 68
ANGELS IN THEIR EYES 70
DEROS 71
ONE MORE TIME 72
1969 IN COUNTRY 74
1969 THE WORLD 76
BODY COUNT 80
NIGHT HOIST MISSION 82
MAIL CALL 84
R & R 86
DEAR JOHN 88
WALKOUT 90
LAST LOOK AROUND 92
FREEDOM BIRD 94
BACK IN THE WORLD 95
ASIAN DREAMS 98
POPPA TANGO SIERRA DELTA 100

VENUS IMPACTED 104
CHOSEN MEN 108
CIVILIANS 110
MEA CULPA 112
571 114
EPITAPH 116
WHAT I LEARNED 118
GLOSSARY OF TERMS 119

ACKNOWLEDGEMENTS

I am grateful for the host of friends who helped me in the writing of this book.

Muchisimas Gracias to my compadre Rick Gallavan for his untiring ear, his patience, guidance and wisdom. Same-same always for Don Avdul, my buddy, mentor and Dustoff brother.

I am indebted to Stu Willis and Steve and Phyllis Cogliano, my Florida family who helped me through the struggle.

I wish to further thank all of the men of the 571st who contributed their time, treasured photographs and mementos.

AIR AMBULANCE UNITS
IN VIETNAM
31 December 1969

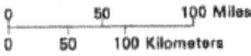

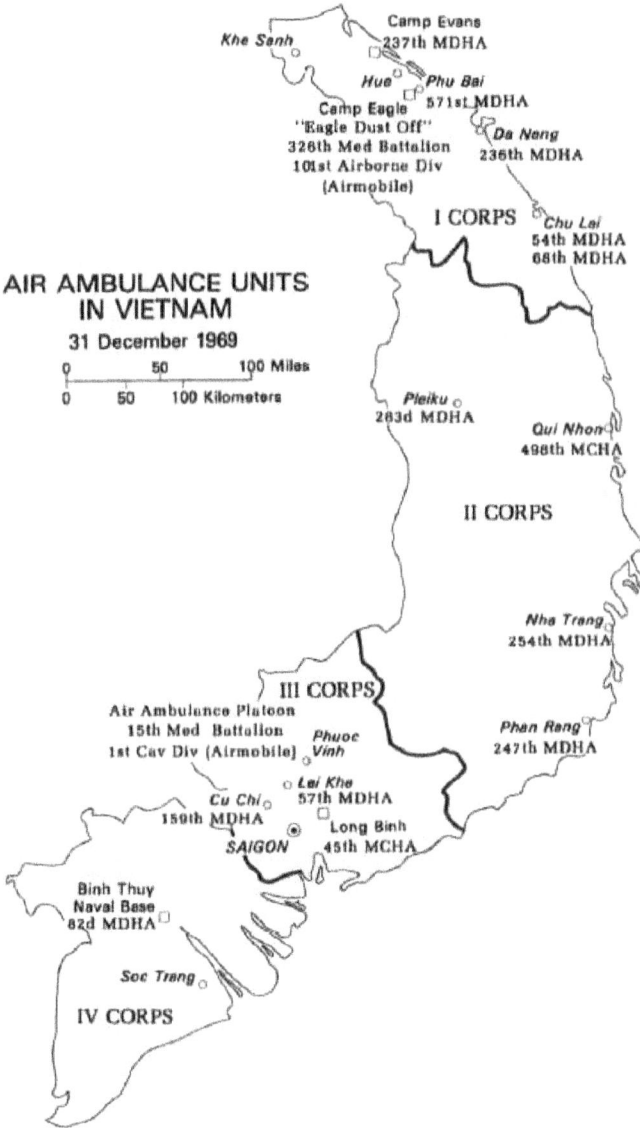

Camp Evans
237th MDHA

Khe Sanh

Hue   Phu Bai
571st MDHA

Camp Eagle
"Eagle Dust Off"
326th Med Battalion
101st Airborne Div
(Airmobile)

Da Nang
236th MDHA

I CORPS   Chu Lai
54th MDHA
68th MDHA

Pleiku
283d MDHA

Qui Nhon
498th MCHA

II CORPS

Nha Trang
254th MDHA

III CORPS

Air Ambulance Platoon
15th Med Battalion
1st Cav Div (Airmobile)   Phuoc
Vinh

Phan Rang
247th MDHA

Lai Khe
57th MDHA

Cu Chi
159th MDHA   Long Binh
45th MCHA

SAIGON

Binh Thuy
Naval Base
82d MDHA

Soc Trang

IV CORPS

PREFACE

At the height of the Vietnam War, the period of mid to late 1969, there were approximately 540,000 American soldiers fighting in Vietnam. They occupied fire bases and compounds scattered throughout the war ravaged country, hemmed in by dense jungle, high mountains, and unforgiving terrain. They were surrounded by a non-uniformed, hostile enemy force living among the civilian populace, revealing themselves only when they attacked and killed, at random, seeking only to inflict maximum casualties and instill maximum terror.

From May of 1962 through March of 1973 approximately 58,000 American men and women soldiers were killed in the fighting. Estimates go as high as 200,000 American wounded. The numbers of civilian casualties during this same period go off the chart, exceeding one million killed on both sides. This was a carnage, spread out over a decade, was the longest sustained war our country has ever fought, and eventually, lost.

By December of 1969 there were fifteen Dustoff Units operating in Vietnam. These small units, usually consisting of six unarmed helicopter ambulances, were positioned throughout the country to provide front line medical evacuation of the wounded to field hospitals. The aim of the Planners of War was that any wounded soldier could be transported to a secure base hospital within thirty minutes. Mostly, this worked.

It was my very great privilege to serve in one of these units, the 571st Medical Detachment, "Phu Bai Dustoff". By coincidence of fate I was the first man assigned to this unit as it formed during the summer of 1967 at Fort Meade, Maryland and I would remain with the 571st for my entire tour in the Army. I would serve 23 of those months in Vietnam where, among my less nefarious duties I flew as a defensive patient protector on rescue missions.

Dustoff units transported an estimated 900,000 patients to hospitals during the course of the war. We units flew an average of four rescue missions a day, every day, for over ten years while suffering a one in three casualty rate among pilots and crew. According to statistics compiled by the Center Of Military History in Washington, D.C. medical evacuation helicopters took hits from enemy gunfire at a rate three times higher than any other military aircraft. On the approximately 8,000 hoist evacuations performed by Dustoff units the rate of enemy fire encountered rose to seven times higher than the in-country average.

What follows is my personal remembrance, a highly subjective history, both of the 571st Dustoff and my experiences in and after Vietnam.

I have written this history in verse, pained at times, because it is my hope that you will read these reflections aloud, hear the military cadence and emotional rhythm of my words in your ears, in your body, and in your heart.

My military journey began in the long ago year of 1967 and continues to this day.

1967

1967, a year of LBJ,
As drums beat on,
Our course was set,
Flagged coffins on the way.

That summer SGT PEPPER
And his Lonely Hearts Club Band
Brought Peace, Love, Dope and Harmony
To the children of the land.

All the fair young maidens
Wore flowers in their hair,
While shot and shell and napalm
Filled Southeast Asia's air.

The year brought the Camaro
And The Monkees on TV,
A Super Bowl for football fans,
A distant DMZ.

While Cool Hand Luke and Bonnie's Clyde
Took us to the show,
The 3rd Mar Div and Flying Cav
Were suffering you know.

It wasn't near as pretty,
No Technicolor there,
Just body bags and bloody rags,
No flowers in their hair.

Despite all this, because I could,
I made my mind up right,
For joining up, for stepping in,
For entering the fight.

I packed my bag with a folded flag,
And orders for my caper,

While they drove off in V-dub vans
And Lots of Zig-zag papers.
Some went to San Francisco
And frolicked in the Haight,
While those of us who heard the call
Got ready for the fight.

Operation Cedar Falls
And one called Junction City,
Bled off our lives and killed our mates,
Daily, without pity.

It was 1967, 50 years ago,
Far past,
When eleven thousands of our soldiers,
Breathed their very last.

American Forces, KIA,
In distant Vietnam.
That year ago, that far-off shore,
Where I went off to see a war.

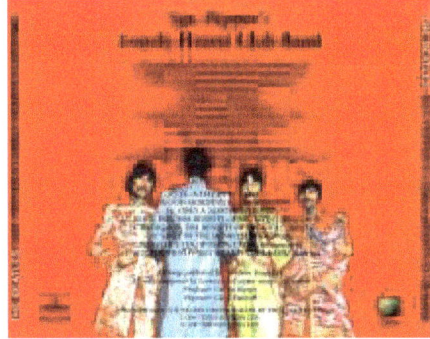

As my past slowly fades to an irrelevant trivia contest, as my touchstones fade, and the here and now becomes ever more baffling, I remember the Sixties as a simpler time, colorful, with feathers and a great soundtrack. They weren't. The Woodstock decade saw the President of our United States assassinated, in broad daylight, sitting next to his wife, in an open convertible, on the downtown streets of Dallas, Texas, during a welcoming motorcade in his honor. Only a week earlier the President of South Vietnam had been assassinated by a coven of military generals who then assumed power. One week, two presidents down.

Let's get this war on the road.

Over the next six years, Lyndon Johnson increased US military presence in Vietnam from 23,000 to over half a million. Over 48,000 of these troops would be killed, another 150,000 wounded. This carnage continued until LBJ announced his intention not to run for reelection, stating he did not want to be the first US President to "lose a war". Richard Nixon had no such reservations. The war churned on. More soldiers died. The sixties ended. The seventies were not going to be much of an improvement. Still there were guitars, fast cars, dense clouds of get you higher smoke, and prosperity. War is ever good business. The sixties were the best of times, the worst of times, depending on who or what you were paying attention to. In March of that year I left my home to enlist in the Army. My adventure had begun.

You can look it up.

D.E.A.D
(Date Entered Active Duty)

I went to Boston, raised my hand,
Pledged allegiance to our land,
My choice to go the Army way,
On March 6th, my enlistment day.

I'd grown so tired of knocking 'round
The sad old streets of my home town.
High school had been such a bore,
What's more exciting than a war?

Just like Davy Crockett,
Marshall Dillon & the rest
I went off to be a hero,
To take the manhood test.

My Dad had been in World War 2,
If he could serve, then I would too.
I'd try to make him proud of me,
And be the man he hoped I'd be.

My Mom, was standing in the door,
As I went off to see a war,
She kissed me though her heart was breaking,
Tears filled her eyes, her hands were shaking.

I couldn't see the cost for them,
As shallow as I was back then,
I only knew it was exciting,
I couldn't wait to join the fighting.

I left them both, my brothers too,
Because I felt my aim was true,
I'd serve my country, get away,
Return a better man one day.

I'd said goodbye to my home town,
And went on my way not crying,
Right now for me it's all a game,
An adventure I'd be trying.

"Let every nation know, whether they wish us well or ill, that we shall pay any price, bear any burden, meet any hardship, support any friend, oppose any foe to assure the survival and success of liberty. This much we pledge and more."

John Fitzgerald Kennedy, Inauguration Speech, 1/20/61.

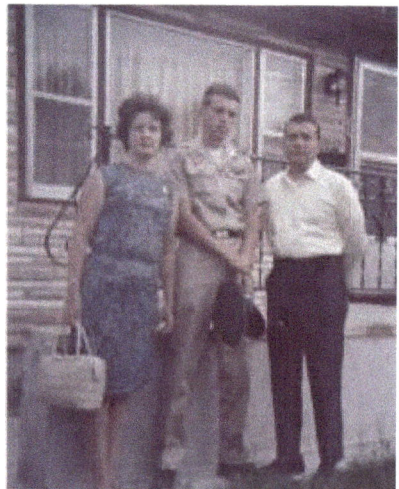

The author with his parents, Jackie and Dave Ferrier, MA, 1967

I let behind my childhood toys,
No more grinning with the boys.
I'd fight for right, I'd be a man,
At least I prayed, I hope I can.

One way or t'other I was going,
While in my heart a notion growing,
I'd go and do the best I could,
And not get killed, knock on wood,

This feels like something I should do,
I can't say why but know its true,
Somewhere in the Army plan
I'll find myself, become a man.

But if I'm wrong and I do die,
And all my childhood dreams go by,
My choice, I made, the Army way,
On March 6th, my enlistment day.

"I, David Owen Ferrier, do solemnly swear that I will support and defend the Constitution of the United States against all enemies, foreign and domestic; that I will bear true faith and allegiance to the same; and that I will obey the orders of the President of the United States and the orders of the officers appointed over me, according to regulations and the Uniform Code of Military Justice. So help me God."

I pledged to give MY LIFE for MY COUNTRY, barely understanding what that truly meant, yet meaning every word of the oath I had taken. I don't know how I could have been less prepared for what would happen next. I was running on faith, on everything I had ever been told, taught, shown or sung to about regarding the history, motivation and good intentions that were, I believed, the cornerstone of the principles of the United States of America.

So off I went. I flew from Boston's Logan Airport to Columbia, South Carolina. First time I'd ever been on an airplane. First time I'd ever been out of New England. Furthest I'd ever been away from my parents, my brothers, my home.

I would spend the next eight weeks of my life at Fort Jackson, South Carolina in Basic Training. This was my life's movie unfolding, and I was the star. Basic Training first, then onward to the war.

B.C.T.
(Basic Combat Training)

Growing up I'd always played
At war games and the like,
But now, at last, I'd made the trade,
A rifle for my bike...

My baseball cap, all Red Sox blue,
I traded for a helmet too,
All made of steel, an Iron Pot,
I really liked it, quite a lot.

Did I mention they cut off all my hair?
No matter how I'd beg,
I looked into a mirror,
My head looked like an egg.

They issued me new clothes all green,
I looked just like a lima bean,
Some that fit, same that didn't
The rest all in-between.

All fun and games,
At least a first,
As sergeants drilled us keen,
But things got grim as weeks rolled by,
Those sergeants, they got mean.

They made it clear,
We weren't worth shit,
That's exactly what they said,
Day in, day out and very loud,
To get it through my head.

At first I didn't think it real,
As they taught me not to feel,
Not to think, or have my say,
Just pull the trigger, just obey.

You're due in Nam the sergeant said,
Pay attention or your dead.

Guys are dying over there,
But never me, that can't be fair,
I'll do everything they say,
I'll play this game the Army way.

We'll kill you here, they'd yell and scream,
To teach me war is not a dream.
Fool around, play and joke,
You'll die in combat's fire and smoke.
This scary point got ever stronger,
I couldn't be a kid much longer.

I spoke new words and awful sounds
To growl amidst the gore,
Motherfucker is a word?
My sister is a whore?

They sounded tough, all that rough talk,
As I trained hard to walk their walk.
I learned to cuss and swear a lot,
And how to sweat when it got hot.

I learned some things that will serve me well
When I go to the Nam,
How to lock and how to load,
And do a lot of harm.

I learned of Jody, he's the guy,
Who'd steal my girl back home,
I heard that if you had a wife,
That she would surely roam.

Don't trust 'em all,
The sergeants said,

A skirts just for a twirl,
A soldier on his way to war
Has no use for a girl.

If the Army had decided,
We need a gal for fun,
They'd shine us up, and line us up
And issue us each one.

At least that's what they told me,
I was sure that they knew more,
Remember I was just a kid
Never away from home before.

So they beat us up,
And beat us down,
Then told us we'd done well
We're Army soldiers after all,
We'd spent our time in hell.

Basis Combat Training,
There I learned the score,
8 weeks after leaving home
Can't be a kid no more.

The Author, Fort Jackson, S.C. 1967

In Basic Training I was surprised by the contempt in which we were held as trainees. I enlisted to become a soldier of my own free will, why were they so mad at me for being there? Why the foul, abusive language? The crudity of it all? American Soldiers should be held to a higher standard.

Why not teach us PRIDE. Congratulate, rather than condemn us? I hadn't done anything WRONG, I thought I'd done what was RIGHT.

Getting ready for a war, preparing to undergo a process where I may have to DIE for my country should have been more dignified, even noble.

Maybe things were going to turn out differently than I imagined they would.

OVER HERE

When I finally finished training
I got orders to a post,
An army camp in Maryland
Where I was needed most.

My hair real short, my khakis new,
I travelled there to see who's who,
I reported in to some dismay,
My unit wasn't there that day.

I was the first, some clerk revealed,
While digging through my file,
He sent me to a barracks,
Said drop by once in a while.

A couple days, then a week,
Went by without a word,
Then that clerk he sent for me
To tell me what he heard.

Five Seven One, my unit name
Was forming on the post
There'd be some guys reporting in
And I would be their host.

He took me to an office
Way off the beaten trail,
I had a phone, a swivel chair
And lots and lots of mail.

The mail was all OFFICIAL,
I put it in a pile,
I swiveled in my swivel chair
And hung around a while.

Then one day I heard a twang,
A sound from in the South,
Asking 'bout Five Seven One
And where to feed his mouth.

Me and Woody made a team
Now called Five Seven One,
Then more guys came, I signed them in,
and nothing much got done.

The days went by,
The mail piled up, I signed for lots of gear
If I had clue what was going on
You wouldn't know it here.

Then one day this guy shows up
A major by his side,
They looked around and shook their heads
I swear they almost cried.

The major said round up the men
Who were scattered 'round the place,
He told me no more foolin' around
With a very solemn face.

I found 'em fast,
Most guys showed up whenever there was chow,
I told them things had changed a bit,
We had a major now.

Our first formation, all in line,
Little better than a mob,
Till Major Vince laid down the law
And told us about our job.

We leave for Nam in 90 days
Maybe a little less
We've got lot of work to do,
And you people are a mess.

Major Vince took control
And got us squared away,
Our 90 days were flying by
It's time to earn our pay.

We packed our stuff and loaded up
A bunch went on a train,
Then Major Vince flew on ahead,
The rest of us remained.

We are pretty ready
Done all we could and more
While waiting for the final word
To fly off to the war.

Now we became unit
A team that works as one
The way that we are shaping up,
That war's as good as won.

Slowly, steadily, I was learning the Army game, assuming responsibility, becoming part of something larger than myself, wanting, earning and gaining the respect of the men in my unit as the days went on.

"Woody" above, is my ever-faithful, good buddy, Larry Woodyard. Woody and I served together in the 571st for two tours in Vietnam. Forty years later, at the first Dustoff reunion I ever attended, Woody was the first person I ran into. Hands down, no doubt, Good Guy. Then and now.

"Major Vince" is our unit's Godfather, first Commanding Officer, mentor, leader and friend, Vince Cedola. More about Vince later.

Vietnam was still a fuzzy green rumor somewhere over the rainbow. I was sure it couldn't be as bad as they said, surely they were just trying to scare us, and besides, if something bad was going to happen surely it wouldn't be happening to me. After all, I was an American soldier, part of an Army that had never known defeat. I realized war was dangerous and that guys were going to be killed and injured. But not me, that was for sure, after all, this was my movie.

So there I was, there we were, whistling not past the graveyard, but while we were walking into it.

THE DUSTOFF MISSION
(Simplified)

A Dustoff Team is comprised of Pilots, Medics, Crew Chiefs, Mechanics, Supply, Radio, and Admin Techs, all volunteers, in support of the Medical Evacuation Mission.

Begin with one DUSTOFF helicopter crew of two pilots, one crew chief, one medic and one patient protector.

They run out to their O.D. colored helicopter that has large red-cross targets painted on the nose and both sides.

They crank up and race out to the battlefield.

Often under a hail of enemy bullets, they land or hover openly in the trees to rescue their precious cargo—the wounded soldier.

They take-off, often still under enemy fire, and provide care and treatment to the wounded, while en-route to the medical facility.

They deliver the soldier into the safe hands of the hospital and fly back to home base.

Then— they clean up their aircraft and prepare to do the same thing again,... and again,... and again,...and again, every day and every night, until their tour of duty is over.

"TO SAVE A LIFE"

Vince Cedola,
LTC, MSC (Ret)
Dustoff 22   82ⁿᵈ MDHA 1964-65
Dustoff 506 571ˢᵗ MDHA 1967-68

GETTING THERE
(Over The Rainbow)

Things are getting serious,
They stuffed us in a plane,
We're off to Nam, right now,
Today, Captain Bob explained

A C-130 cargo plane,
The kind that has no seats,
We squatted down against the walls,
With cargo at our feet.

East Coast to West the prop plane ride,
Hours and hours stuffed inside
California here we come,
With all our asses getting numb.

If we looked real fast
We got to see, Hawaii,
Hula State
But not for long, back in the air
Flying with the freight.

Mactan Island, Philippines
The next place that we stopped
Three days so far inside the plane
Over islands that we hopped.

Japan from there, the final pause,
And though it makes no sense,
We couldn't wait to get to Nam,
The boys were getting tense.

Four days in a cargo plane,
The kind that has no seats,
No restrooms and no stewardess,
And really lousy eats.

Nha Trang at last,
We landed,
In the middle of the night,
They dropped the ramp,
We trundled out,
A very sorry sight.

The SMELL at first, Oh my God,
That pungent Asian rot,
And then THE HEAT who would'a thought?
The middle of the stinking night,
Could be so stinking hot.

Vince was there, he'd flown ahead,
With our first party crew
With Harry G, some other guys,
I don't remember who.

So we touched down
And sniffed around
And then a special treat
We said goodbye to that old plane
The one that had no seats.

The whole plane ride was a lark, a stepping off into the great adventure. Granted it got pretty monotonous by day 3 and downright uncomfortable a day before that, but the THRILL was there, the excitement of going to see the elephant.

"Captain Bob" is Robert Peneguy, Movement Officer, Flyboy, Good Guy.

"Harry G" is Harry Geist, Medic, Buddy, whereabouts unknown.

We were still whistling and we had landed in the graveyard.

DEPARTMENT OF THE ARMY
571st MEDICAL DETACHMENT (HELICOPTER AMBULANCE)
Fort George G. Meade, Maryland 20755

18 October 1967

The following named personnel are scheduled for deployment with the 571st Medical Detachment (Helicopter Ambulance):

NAME	RANK	SN
Cedola, Vincent J	MAJ	078678
Naylor, Donald L	MAJ	076460
Peneguy, Robert O	1LT	02326063
Duncan, Chester E	CW2	W3152460
Barrows, Robert J	WO1	W3157004
Elliott, William H	WO1	W3157063
Fisher, Gene L	WO1	W3157059
Funk, Ellsworth D	WO1	W3157073
Safrit, Merlin G	WO1	W3157176
Terry, Bruce A	WO1	W3155144
Vandever, John H	WO1	W3157212
Williams, Willie K	SSG	RA14599947
Adair, James J	SGT	RA14778101
Walley, Robert L	SP/5	RA14594808
Yost, Roger E	SP/5	RA51503132
Peters, Michael V	SP/4	US51797859
Barone, Thomas M	PFC	RA11815586
Cook, William J	PFC	US52685251
Cox, Stephen	PFC	RA11961353
Cryer, Kenneth O	PFC	RA11756926
Ferrier, David O	PFC	RA11620502
Geist, Harry	PFC	RA11860719
Hill, Albert S	PFC	RA14508307
Kirk, Johnie	PFC	RA18843263
McLaughlin, Dwight L	PFC	US51592215
Salvatore, Mario A	PFC	US51513257
Tripp, George L	PFC	RA10852160
Wade, James D	PFC	RA11704913
Woodyard, Larry	PFC	RA11607672

VINCENT J CEDOLA
MAJ, MSC
Commanding

IN COUNTRY
(Nha Trang, November 1967)

Okay, we're here,
We look around,
Lots of frightening sights,
Sandbags, barbed wire, lots of guns
And flares that light the night.

The heat is hot, the air is foul,
Lots of strange new smells,
We have no idea where the bad guys are,
And no one ever tells.

The Vietnamese all look skinny,
And very, very poor,
The ones that aren't afraid of us
Make us fear them even more.

They're burning shit beside the road,
There are no sewers here,
We just heard they put formaldehyde
Into the local beer.

The old folks all have black teeth
From chewing betel nut,
Another funny local habit
These crazy Asians got.

There's Vespa cabs and Saigon Tea
For us to ride and buy
Pretty girls who go for twirls
And gunships in the sky.

The chow's not bad, the water stinks,
The hospital's overflowing,
The wounded guys in their blue duds
Know something we're not knowing.

All in all so far so good
Been here one whole day,
I'm guessin' I can handle this
If things should go my way.

First day in Nam there is no doubt
It's time to see the light,
I may not make it through the year
But I will try with all my might.

It was all so exotic, so DIFFERENT from anything, anywhere I'd ever been, anything I'd ever seen, or heard, or smelled or tasted. I wasn't scared yet. I was Alert, Cautious, Curious, and above all else, Exhilarated! Some inner sense told me it was time to stop whistling, but the sense of Adventure has only heightened. Of course none of us had heard the alarm bells, the sirens…

In hindsight I'm amazed at how NAÏVE, how unprepared we were, I was. Naïve covers a lot of ground when you are young.

The lights were slowly coming on as we settled into garrison life at Nha Trang airfield, a big city, a big airport, which looked safe to me and nobody around me looked particularly worried.

The 8th Field Hospital was adjacent to our barracks however and held huge numbers of wounded soldiers from "out there", wherever that was. Mortuary trucks delivered corpses like milkmen to refrigerated containers where they were kept until they were shipped home. Best not to dwell too long on what that was all about.

As we flew training missions with a veteran Dustoff unit we saw the countryside outside our perimeter, LOTS of bomb craters, eerie looking smoke rising from smoldering tree lines, bloody bandages and blank stares on the wounded we picked up.

Perhaps this trip wasn't going to be so easy after all.

HÃY YÊU MẾN
QUÊ HƯƠNG
TỔ-QUỐC

CÁC EM LÀ
RƯỜNG CỘT TƯƠNG-
LAI CỦA NƯỚC
NHÀ

I saw thousands of these during my tour in Vietnam. Didn't know what it said then, don't know what it says now

FIVE ZERO SIX
(1967-1969)

506, The man in charge,
The leader of our pack,
The best of us he had to be,
Or we weren't coming back.

Vince was first, he got us there,
The States to Vietnam,
He shaped us up, a bunch of kids,
To keep us safe from harm.

The best of us, without a doubt,
He got us in, he got us out,
Vince raised our standard to the Max,
And always, always had our backs.

Vince Cedola, "506",
1967-1968

Dave was next, a gentleman,
A leader blessed with grace,
He taught us to be better men,
In a very bloody place.

On Dave's watch our unit knew
There's no one better at what we do,
No mission ever turned aside,
No wounded without Dustoff's ride.

Dave Dryden,
"506", 1968-1969

They bore the burden, took the weight,
Held the wheel, healed our Fate,
They led our unit without fuss,
And always were the best of us.

Dave Dryden, Vince Cedola,
Commander USS Repose, South
China Sea, 1968

Without these two men I would have a much different story to tell. Vince Cedola and Dave Dryden were calm, patient, and immensely tolerant of the teenagers they led. Both men LED by example, with an understanding hand which made the incomprehensible, tolerable.

FLYBOYS

They sat up front and flew the ship.
In a plastic bubble, hip to hip,
Low and fast, high and tight,
Day in, day out, through darkest night.

Vince and Dave, Ken and Pete,
Side by side in the pilot's seat.
They got us there and got us out,
With lives we saved without a doubt.

Stu and Willie, Carl and Bob,
No better at the Dustoff job,
Bill and Gary, Jim & Jack,
They flew us out and flew us back.

Mark & Chester, John & Fred,
They flew our ships,
They braved the dread,
Nothing turned them back you know,
With wounded on the ground below.

Those whose names were called out here,
Gather with us, year to year,
As we look back on what we've done,
As we fly toward our setting sun.

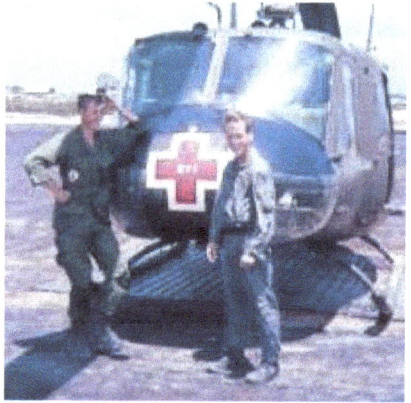

Bob Peneguy, John
Chisholm, Flyboys
Phu Bai, 1968

Stu Willis, unkown,
Phu Bai, 1968

Pete Leonard, "Checking his
Six", Phu Bai, 1969

Many more our Dustoff's flew,
AC's, pilots, the best we knew,
Dustoff's Mission,
Dustoff's Pledge,
These flyboys were our living edge.

Dustoff pilots, a breed apart,
They flew our ships with gallant hearts.
The last they'd never, ever say,
These finest men from Dustoff's day.

Stu Willis, Willie Jackson,
Flyboys, Phu Bai, 1968

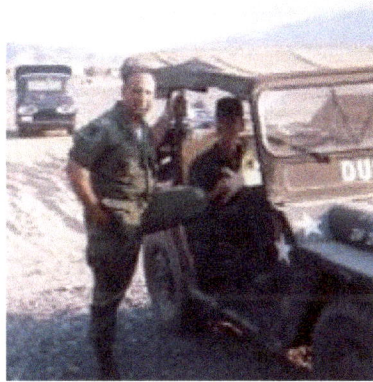

Vince Cedola, Chet
Duncan, Nha Trang, 1967

Flyboys Award Ceremony, Phu Bai, 1968

Pilots. They really were a distinct breed. At the controls, in the air they were phenomenal, the best. Ten feet away from the aircraft they were, like us, two or three year's older, maybe, but just as overwhelmed, homesick, uncertain and scared, until they were flying again. Then they were Flyboys. None better.

CHERRY BOYS
(For Don, my buddy)

Cherry boys, so very young,
So with that nickname we are hung,
Baby-sans, another way,
They make their point, and have their say.

Our fighting allies, Vietnamese,
Each and every one who sees,
America, the Land of Might,
Has sent its children off to fight.

Cherry boys, that name's not right,
At 18 we make quite a sight,
We carry guns for killing here,
Though back home we can't buy a beer.

It's also only fair to note,
At 18 we're too young to vote,
We're old enough to kill, they think,
But not enough to have a drink.

We're plenty old for night patrol.
With our heads all full of rock & roll,
And though we might look like a child,
Don't be around when we get riled.

The Army taught us how to kill,
And sent us where they hope we will,
But underneath those woeful ploys,
We're still 18, Cherry Boys.

We coulda' used a few more years,
Of hanging around our high school peers,
Instead they shipped us off to war,
Guess that's what Cherry Boys are for.

Children, all of us, growing up fast, but not fast enough. War is swift.

(Front sitting) Ray Barnett, Don Avdul
(2nd Row) Left to Right Larry Woodyard, Steve Cogliano, "Reb" Pearson, Henry Birchall, Hank Adams, Author
(3rd Row) Standing, left to right, Larry Gilland, George Washington, Danny "Supply" Hidalgo, unknown
(Back Row) Just the heads, Gary Ball, Johnnie Kirk, Vladmir Fofanoff

THE GOOD GUYS

We saw civilians pushed around,
Smacked in the face, knocked to the ground,
Sometimes women, sometimes men,
Even children now and then.

Ground troops messing with the locals,
Peasants, farmers, Vespa Yokels,
Didn't always seem okay,
Yet it happened every day.

White Mice we called the VN cops,
Stood around at traffic stops,
Frisked the ladies, shook the guys,
No hint of mercy in their eyes.

Our own MP's a little better,
At their tough job done to the letter,
"Check your papers if you please"
Wasn't easy being Vietnamese.

You couldn't always see the ones
Who walked around with hidden guns?
Who might just drop a live grenade,
Or poison you with lemonade.

Better to be safe than sorry,
Better hunter than the quarry,
And if they had done nothing wrong,
Growl at them to move along.

The problem with the whole damn scheme,
It was built upon a fearful dream,
Of babies wired to explode,
Of soldiers dying in the road.

Just no time to treat them fair,
Charley could be anywhere,
Women, children, teenage kids,
If they talked back we flipped our lids.

Just too bad if they got sore,
Those were the rules in this rough war.
Didn't make us many friends,
Yet it seemed to meet our ends.

To be a good guy in the Nam,
Meant sometime facing extra harm,
Wear your white hat if you must
But be careful who you trust,

You try to treat these people nice,
Your body may go home on ice.
So be a good guy if you dare,
Charley can be anywhere.

Advice and experience accumulating like scar tissue as the Fear Factor increased, rumors abounded, resentments built, labeling got easier. The war machine at work, and working well.

IS THAT GUY DEAD?
(December, 1967)

Some action on the berm last night,
At least we heard the fire,
Tracers in and tracers out,
Gooks were in the wire.

That's what some guy told us
In the mess hall eating chow,
So we finished up our powdered eggs
To see if they're there now.

We grabbed a jeep and rode out where
The barbed wire held us in,
Where deadfall lines and claymore mines
Scarred the earth and tore the skin.

There were some sentries poking 'round
All gunned up in their wrath
Pointing at a pile of rags
Blown about in half.

Is that guy dead? My voice did say,
Dumber than the rest.
You couldn't bleed that much and live,
And look, he's got no chest!

We looked real hard and all could see
His pink and bloody lungs
Hanging in the barbed wire fence,
Dripping from the rungs.

Okay, enough, we'd seen the gore,
A human being smashed by war,
Yet we couldn't look away
We might end up like that someday.

On the jeep ride going back
Nobody spoke of the attack,
First dead guy we'd seen for real
A lesson learned in not to feel.

Better not to wonder who
You'd rather see be dead than you.
Let him stay there, let him lie,
Don't look too close when passing by,

Still had a lot of tour to go,
Dead bodies won't be rare you know
Best to keep them from your sight
If you ever want to sleep at night.

Is that guy dead? Just look, don't see,
Next time could be you or me
Hanging in the bloody wire
Burning on the funeral pyre.

Yeah, this happened, not just to me, but to everybody, sooner or later, in one form or another.

This changed me. I hadn't seen things like this on TV or in the movies. Maybe this wasn't going to be my movie after all.

GOOKS

Gooks or slopes or dinks and such,
Didn't matter very much,
As long as they weren't people-fied,
Made it easier when they died.

Baby-sans or Victor Charlie,
Dropped like leaves when things got gnarly,
Ragged shapes, never look at faces,
Bloody rags in bloody places.

Gooks was good,
The word is sly,
Not much there to Personify.
Couldn't have them being real,
Drop one then that hurt won't heal.

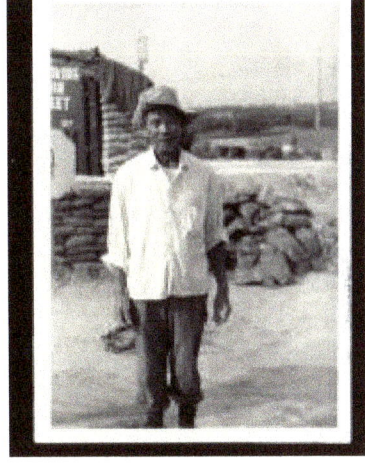

Poppa San, Phu Bai, 1969

Gooks or slopes or dinks, back then,
Better that than call them men.
But once we learned that trick's not true,
We killed them still, Red, White & Blue.

We killed them till the war did end,
And now to you this message send.
Niggers, spics, rag-heads too.

The trick don't work, we tell you true.
'Cause wars will be, and never end,
Till Gooks and slopes and dinks are men.

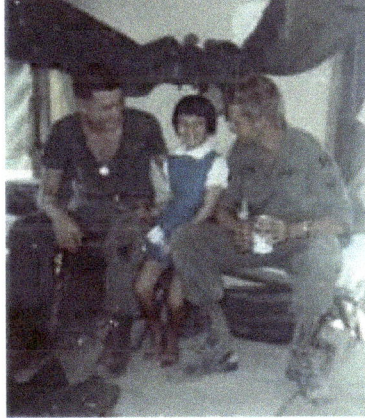

Harry Geist, young evac-
uee, the Author

Amen

NAM STUFF
(Talkin' Trash)

Boonie hats, short timers sticks,
Papa-sans, boom-boom tricks,
Saigon tea and mess hall chow,
C-rat smokes and dinky-dau,
R&R and M-16's
Bob Hope shows and beauty queens.

Poppin' smoke and bought the farm,
Smokin'dope and Baum-me Baum.
Poncho liners, combat boots,
K-bar knives & Nomex suits.

Getting short and getting ready,
Homesick blues and staying steady.
Terrified with frozen fear,
Nasty drunk with piss warm beer.

Hooch mate pals who became our brothers,
Lifelong bonds with one another.
Mail from home, strong friendship built,
Sorrow deep, Survivor Guilt.

Combat pay and fire bases,
Burning shit and death card aces.
365 and home alive,
Our bags were packed with all that jive.

We spoke our own rough language then.
Man to man, friend to friend,
It made the war seem all less real,
It gave us something less to feel.

The indescribably beautiful Ann Margaret,
Bob Hope Tour, Christmas 1968

Humping Ruck, Nam, Everyday

We learned very little Vietnamese, barely a word, never a sentence. We expected, demanded, that they understand us, even though we sometimes barely understood ourselves.

This new language was a compromise, a mutual tongue for the native folk and us. We taught them, they taught us. The more I spoke it the more acclimated I became, the further from home I got. The new normal wasn't, I was losing sight of where I came from, getting used to who I was, saying goodbye forever to the guy with the head like an egg who looked just like a lima bean.

1968
(In Country)

The year roared in with Big Tet's fight,
The cities burned, night after night,
Saigon, Cholon, Danang & Hue,
Every Fire Base, every day.

In Bitter Time we drove them out,
Of every post they sought to rout,
We settled back and with much dread,
We counted up our New Year's Dead.

A thousand plus five hundred more,
KIA, the US score,
Piles and piles of VC dead,
Tens of thousands so they said.

The year wore on, more men went under,
Khe Sanh's siege & Rolling Thunder,
A Shau valley's Arc Light strikes,
We stacked their dead on paddy dikes.

In My Lai village we found shame,
Though fear and hatred were to blame,
The breakdown was our honor lost,
In '68 part of the cost.

A tough old year was '68,
We who lived it mark its date,
The bloodiest of the whole damn war,
16 Thousand Killed and more.

I only know that's what they say,
But to make our dead add up that way,
50 soldiers died every day.
In '68, the price we'd pay.

This was my 1968. Crystal clear, immediate, undimmed by time.

1968
(The World)

In '68 back in the States
They were having quite a party,
Laugh In had come on the air
With Dan and Dick and Artie.

The Beatles sang about Hey Jude
And want a Revolution,
RFK and MLK died seeking a solution.

Our Navy lost the Pueblo ship
And all the men she carried,
Elvis had a baby girl
And Johnny Cash got married.

LBJ gave up his post
After due reflection,
Decided the Asian war was lost
And bad for reelection.

Oh yeah, that war in Vietnam.
They watched it every night,
A kind of sad TV show,
Hosted by Cronkite.

Apollo 8 went round the moon,
And Star Trek hit the air,
The Mick hit his last Home Run
And Broadway gave them Hair.

'68 what a blast,
If you weren't where the blasting
Was blowing us to Kingdom come,
And Heaven everlasting.

This was someone else's year. Everything I know about this 1968 I learned second hand. I saw and knew of it only through the haze of Vietnam. I still resent the good things I missed, if I missed any good things at all.

ANYTIME, ANYPLACE
(Anywhere)

Sandbagged hooches, barbed wire fences,
Claymore mines and deep slit trenches,
Mortar rounds, fuel dump fire,
Punji stakes, concertina wire.

Checkpoints, guard dogs, tense MP's
Floating flares and DMZ's
Typhoid, Typhus, Cholera too,
Lots of shots for me and you.

Cobras, kraits, bamboo vipers,
Tigers, rats and hidden snipers,
Bulldozed berms and free fire zones,
Tunnels deep and rotting bones.

Poisoned beer and dogs with rabies,
Plague all over little babies,
Grave yards blasted, shattered crosses,
Killed the poor ones, killed the bosses.

Didn't matter who you were,
He or she, him or her,
In the jungle, in the rear,
Death was always lurking near.

Twilight, nighttime, breaking dawn,
Noontime, dinner, Dead and Gone,
In an instant, without warning,
Every night and every morning.

Try not to see it,
Turn your head,
Take a break,
You end up dead.

Bad old Nam, right in your face,
Anytime, Anyplace.

The red lights are all on now, the alarm bells never stop ringing. No spit to whistle.

HUE IN FLAMES
(Going North, February 1968)

Right in the middle of Tet's big fight,
With battles raging day and night,
New orders came for our whole gang,
We're moving North, above Da Nang.

What the hell? We just got here,
Got used to drinking iced down beer,
We heard the further North you'd go,
Charlie Cong ran the show.

Up North was for Marines and such,
Nobody liked it very much,
Conveniences were pretty rare
And there was LOTS of fighting there.

Phu Bai Helipad and
hooches, 1969
Home Sweet Home

It's not like we had a lot of say
In where we'd be or where we'd stay,
So off we went, goodbye Nha Trang,
We're moving North, above Da Nang.

Phu Bai was our destination,
The place we'd settle down,
But first there was a problem there,
A swamp was all around.

The Seabees came and dropped some sand
Where we would pitch our tents,
They sprayed some oil that smelled real bad
And that became our helipad.

We settled in, it rained a lot,
But the fighting here was very hot,
Those Mud Marines fought like they'd learned
And down the road Hue City burned.

The NVA held the city
And killed its people without pity,
They were dug in with heavy guns,
Killed all the priests and all the nuns.

Hundreds thrown in shallow graves,
Hue's people slain in bloody waves,
Those Mud Marines were fighting mad
They attacked the walls with all they had.

We fetched their wounded from the fight,
They took the city with their might.
Dead civilians everywhere
The NVA had killed them there.

Then slipped away into the night
Past ARVN troops who wouldn't fight,
They fled into the jungles where
We'd have to go and kill them there.

Welcome to the I Corp fight,
A bloody brawl for freedom's right,
No more drinking iced down beer
The war up here would last all year.

Phu Bai was the far away boonies when we got there. War up front and personal. Mortar attacks, rocket attacks, often, WAY too often.

The wounded poured into the brand new 22nd Surgical Hospital, with its inflatable rubber wards. Limping men in blue pajamas everywhere. There was nowhere to look that the war was not right in front of you.

In Hue City there was a massacre, My Lai squared, mass graves, dead school children, random executions. The North Vietnamese Army held the city for ten days and during that time slaughtered large numbers of the civilians trapped in the city. A lot of this didn't make the evening news, never sure why. I guess you had to be there. We were.

INCOMING
(Things Go Boom)

Incoming rounds, those crunching sounds,
False thunder, flashing light,
Tore up our dreams and midnight schemes
Sent us scurrying in the night.

Our enemy he got in close
To fire his rockets steep,
He spread his fire inside our wire
To kill us in our sleep.

The first round jars us from our beds
Someone gives a shout,
Then three or four and sometime more
Spread havoc all about.

Fire in the Night (Again),
Phu Bai, 1969

A mad dash to the bunkers where
Sandbagged walls will give protection
Then wait it out while react teams
Spread out in each direction.

The booming done we venture out
To check to see who's screaming
The guys struck down before they had
A chance to stop their dreaming.

The excitement dims, we all calm down
Then go back to our beds
No more shooting, at least for now
Except inside our heads.

Now rest is gone, no chance of sleep
After a night attack
We lay awake and wonder when
The bombs are coming back.

Not every night, but often enough. Looking back I have no idea how I slept at all in that place. I'm positive, even today, I could recognize that incoming round apart from all other sounds, and most of the time I can't even hear my telephone ring.

HOT LZ's
(Without Ducking)

When battles raged without a break,
And injured men were dying,
A call to get their wounded out
Meant Dustoff would be flying.

Landing zones still taking fire,
With wounded to evac,
Meant get in quick and get out slick
Or no one's coming back.

Of course we knew of danger close
And feared incoming shot,
But this is the job we chose to do
In LZ's that were hot.

While flying in we'd call for guns,
That's gunships by the way,
To hover round and scorch the ground,
Drive the enemy away.

We'd come in high till we got close
Then skim right through the fight,
And land right where the wounded lay,
And start to put things right.

Once we were down, the best approach,
Point our tail boom at the fire,
Load the wounded on the ship
Then get us back up higher.

So we'd hop to get the injured in,
Lay 'em out, strap them tight,
With bullets popping everywhere
And the enemy in sight.

Best not to think about the guns
Firing at our crew,
Nor bullet holes that nicked our souls,
As near misses always do.

Things move fast, a lot of moving parts to get this done,
If all of us kept all our cool,
A little victory won.

When the ground was clear, or our ship full
We'd clamber back aboard
And fly fast out to that safe place where
Medicine was stored.

We'd turn 'em over to the Doc's
And get our ship back ready
Cause flying men from hot LZ's
In Nam that work was steady.

Gunsight clear, in retrospect, a whizzing blur while it was happening. I recall the after, when we were back at our base, how my hands would shake, how I gulped for air, how hard I tried not to let anybody see me doing this.

Popping Smoke.
Vietnam, Anywhere

CASUALTIES
(Ours)

When our men started getting shot
While flying missions that were hot
It left a gap, an empty slot
Right in our hearts as on we fought.

You see once any man went down,
He's whisked away to Medic Town,
Some hospital quite far away,
Never to come back our way.

One minute here, the next he's not,
Just his gear, that's not a lot,
When wounded friends are on your mind,
And sadness is what is left behind.

You know he's getting the best of care,
And that he's being taken where,
There is neither shot nor shell
To hound him while he's getting well.

You're glad he's wounded, didn't die,
You're happy Death has passed him by,
But all that doesn't help a lot
As you fold your buddy's empty cot.

Suddenly there's one less guy,
To count on as the time goes by,
Your tour's a little more alone,
A parting that you can't postpone.

Maybe he'll write back in time,
But if not, it's not a crime,
His head is better not in this place
As he tries to rejoin the human race.

This happens with each wounded man,
We handle it as best we can,
Best not to dwell on who's not here,
When pushing back the daily fear.

The message that the wounded send
Is long before our tour will end
We could end up getting shot
As buddies fold our empty cot.

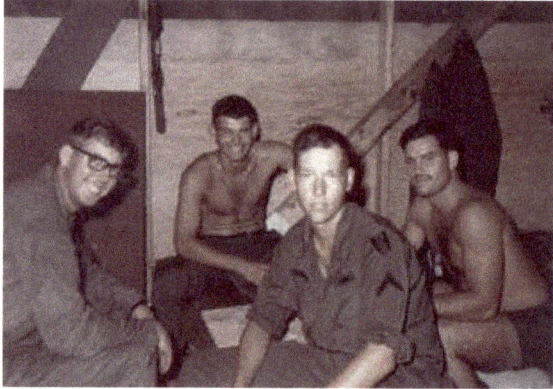

Foreground with shirts: Bob Byrd, Dave Comer,
Dustoff Medics, Good Guys. We folded both their
cots. Rear shirtless: Dusty Rhodes, Will Skoal

Instant denial, instant amnesia, furtive glances, quick peeks, stay busy, talk
about something else, move on, face forward. Don't scream.

FOX MIKE RADIO, MIDNIGHT SHIFT
(Answered Prayers)

Late night radios, one man alone,
Man's his post by combat's phone,
No violent calls so far this night,
Until a Red and Flashing light...

Phu Bai Dustoff, Phu Bai Dustoff,
Makin Taxi Victor. Over.
Taxi Victor, Phu Bai, Go.

Suddenly the silence broken,
From the jungle, softly spoken,
Taxi Victor in the bush,
Is calling us on Evac Push.

Roger, Phu Bai,
I have an emergency med-evac,
2 US, Gunshot Wounds, Litter,
1 US, Gunshot Wound, Ambulatory.

A cry for mercy in the night,
3 men had fallen in the fight,
Now for us to get them clear,
To bring them to safe haven here.

Taxi Victor, Phu Bai, Wait One.

First up is called,
The LZ found,
For Taxi Victor on the ground,
Tac Push next, then skids light,
Five men from Dustoff off in flight

Makin Taxi Victor, Dustoff Five Zero Two...
Zero Two, Taxi Victor, Go...
I am inbound your Poz, ETA Two Zero minutes.
Please advise last enemy contact.

Taxi Victor tells us sure,
The LZ's safe, the ground secure.
Will mark with strobes and light the night,
Will advise when we're in sight.

Meanwhile back at Dustoff's base,
The men awake and take their place,
In, around the radio shack
To watch and wait till our men get back.

Lots of whispers, nervous glances,
Cigarettes and anxious dances
No man is glad he's left behind,
We're all aboard in our own mind.

Makin Taxi Victor, Dustoff Five Zero Two...
Five Zero Two, Taxi Victor, Go...
We have your lights,
Ready your wounded.

A whomping swoop, a flood of light,
The jungle shines, far too bright,
The wounded groan as placed inside,
Our ship lifts off, the homeward ride.

Plasma Hotel, Dustoff Five Zero Two...
Zero Two, Plasma Hotel, Go...
I am inbound with three US Gunshot wounds,
ETA Two Zero...
Five Zero Two, Plasma Hotel, Roger.

Within an hour our ship is back,
Our men return to sleeping racks,
And all alone by combat's phone,
Our radio man sits all alone,
Waiting for another flight,
A cry for mercy in the night.

More Fire in the Night (Every Night)

A routine mission, on a routine night, nobody got hurt, nothing went wrong, everybody got home safe. We flew hundreds, even thousands of these.

A side fact, on this Fox Mike Mission, like many others, no one, neither the radio operator, nor the whole flight crew was over 25 years old.

The 571st Medical Detachment, like all of the Vietnam Dustoff units, would plan, execute and complete missions such as this every day, every night, completely on our own. TO SAVE A LIFE.

KIA
(All)

Killed In Action, a shallow tag,
Put our buddies in a bag,
Each one dead, a KIA,
Each one died a different way.

Chucky got it in the head,
Max while lying in his bed,
Paul while humping on patrol,
Don in his own fighting hole.

Stan and Mike, Josh and Phil,
When their chopper hit a hill,
Steve, and this one's really crazy,
Steve got killed 'cause he was lazy.
Left his flak vest on his rack,
Took two bullets in the back.

Trask, some butter-bar LT,
Died from shrapnel in the knee.
They didn't get the bandage tight,
He bled out slowly in the night.

I heard Cooper flat OD'd,
On med-pac morphine that he'd thieved,
Lacy got squashed by a truck,
Talk about some rotten luck.

I didn't see each man here die,
Just heard about it,
By and by.
You see it went on every day,
In every place, in every way.

For war will always have its price,
Though it never kills the same man twice,
As each man fell, we'd silent pray,
Please don't let them tag me KIA.

Self-preservation was a very private, very secret ritual. Seeing, smelling, touching the grotesquely dead bodies of young men like ourselves was beyond, way beyond, any coping mechanism I ever imagined having. After the desperation, after the terror subsided it was best to feel nothing at all, as quickly as possible. I may have been too lost, too helpless, too overwhelmed by everything going on around me to know what I wanted or how I could attain those wants but I did know one thing above all others, I DIDN'T WANT TO BE DEAD. And of course, I realized, through my despair that neither did they.

BETTER HIM THAN ME
(A Personal Lament)

Hail Mary, full of grace,
And other supplications,
The secret prayers I'd silent say,
Defying explanations.

To ward off ghosts, to keep me strong,
To make me feel less stranded,
But most of all I'd pray them when
With wounded we had landed.

A soldier with a blown off leg,
Or a bullet in his belly,
Just thinking he could be me,
Turned my legs to jelly.

Better him than me I'd whimper,
Never very loud,
A coward's code, pathetic plea,
By brave men not allowed.

To hold a man in mortal pain,
And in his eyes see dying,
Took all I had to hold the line,
And keep myself from crying.

And when his life did flicker out,
His ragged last breath taken,
Better him than me I sobbed
As shameful thoughts awaken.

So I feel shame, and deep regret,
And will for all my days,
A coward's brand only I can see,
For each time in my heart I'd plea,
Better him, Dear God, than me.

Not just me, my buddies, my crewmates the doctors, nurses, clergymen who dealt with the dead and wounded every day whispered this shameful prayer in silence as well. Everyone gets a broken heart, and there's no self-forgiveness in the middle of the night.

WRITING HOME
(I'm Still Alive)

Dear Mom & Dad is how I'd start,
And then begin the hardest part,
Of what to say or tell them true
About this place and what I do.

Of course I tell them I am well,
There is no need to worry,
I ask about the dogs and cats
And keep the hard facts blurry.

They tell me that they saw the news
And what they saw was scary,
I tell them that's all far away,
There's nothing here that's hairy.

I tell them that I sit and type,
And get the mail and such,
I tell them almost any tale,
But I never tell them much.

The bad stuff I store deep inside,
No use in my folks knowing
How deep in me the fear resides,
And how much it is growing.

So I write a bit and tell white lies,
And keep the letters flowing,
No easy task lest truth be told
Of how this war is going.

No need for stamps,
The postage's free,
This Army life is bitchin'
No need to scare them half to death
When they read this in their kitchen.

I truthfully do not recall what on God's green earth I could have written about
during my tour in Vietnam. I know I wrote, the correspondence has not survived.
I wish I could hear what my voice was then, perhaps that would help me understand the voice I speak in now.

DON'T MEAN NOTHIN'
(But It Did)

Don't mean nuthin,
Hear me pray,
This was my mantra
Day by day.

When a buddy fell
Beneath the wheel
Don't mean nuthin
The way to feel.

Gunshot wounds, mortar rounds,
Arc light strikes as thunder sounds,
Frozen fear, my blood like ice,
Don't mean nuthin, or pay the price.

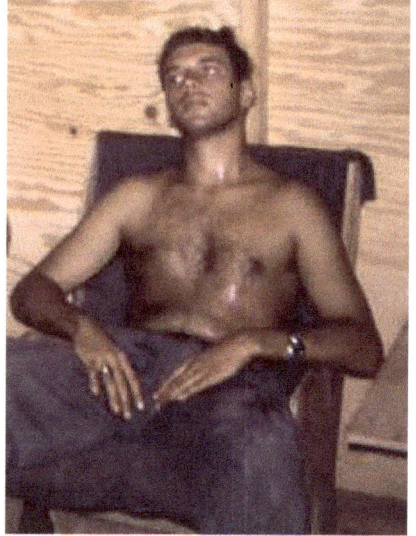

The Author (sweating)

Horrors here, terrors there,
Death surrounds me, everywhere,
Don't mean nuthin,
Take a breath,
Don't mean nuthin',
Dance with Death.

It was all about my brain shut down,
So not to see what's all around,
Try not to feel the aching pain,
Don't mean nuthin', once again.

Don't mean nuthin',
Hear me pray,
Just let me survive another day.

Really, really getting lost now, sinking into the pit, no longer fighting the suction. Daily life is all mud and blood, hot and cold, trudging forward, head down, keeping promises, sharing the load, not looking up too often.

MORE NAM STUFF

Donut Dollies, FNG's
REMFS and ROKS and RPGS
Cherry boys, beaucoup ti-ti,
Arc Light, bloopers, catching Z's

Sucking chests and T&T's
Multiple frags and hot LZ's
Beehive rounds and Willie Pete,
Humping ruck and jungle feet.

Loaches, Cobras APCs,
Puff or Smoky bringing pee,
Di-di mau and lock and load,
Blessings sent and blessings owed.

Hank Adams, Phu Bai, 1969

Chieu Hoi, Xin Loi, Please Bac-si,
Snake and Nape and H&E,
Body bags and med-evacs,
Cutting trail on jungle tracks.

Same-same me and same-same you,
Saigon, Da Nang & Pleiku.

No longer strange, these words ring clear,
As we amend our language here,
No longer us so far away
We're right at home with what we say.

Our new words conceal our feelings,
Help us with our daily dealings,
Numbah One and Numbah Ten,
Strange new words for strange new men.

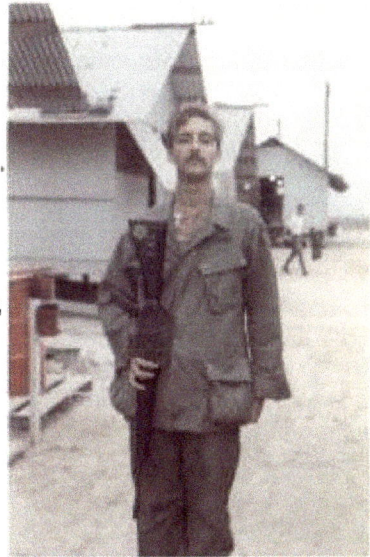

Phil Rugen, Phu Bai, 1969

Our new language, our new thoughts, grown more complex as we drifted further away from who we used to be. The new words help define the new us, our new Native Tongue.

HONOR WITHOUT MEDALS

Courage is a humble deed,
Not always forged in fire,
A simple act, a burden born,
Can serve a purpose higher.

On every day in Vietnam
And throughout every night
We had to do what we had to do
To get our jobs done right.

Cooks who rose before the dawn
To light the mess hall fires,
Artillerymen and RTO's,
Mechanics changing tires.

Clerks who saw that we got paid,
Bakers for the bread they made,
Nurses when our wounds they'd tend,
Surgeons as our limbs they'd mend.

Fuel dump workers, fearsome places,
That often blew up in their faces,
Airfield guards and convoy squads,
Chaplains praying to their gods.

Seabees building unmined roads,
Drivers hauling crucial loads,
Mailmen healing with the mail,
Sailors with their ships to sail.

Each soldier at his work each day,
No matter where, in any way,
Braved the struggle, took his chance,
That Death would interrupt his dance.

Duty done and honor bright
Served us all within the fight
Promises made to do one's best
Put each man's courage to the test

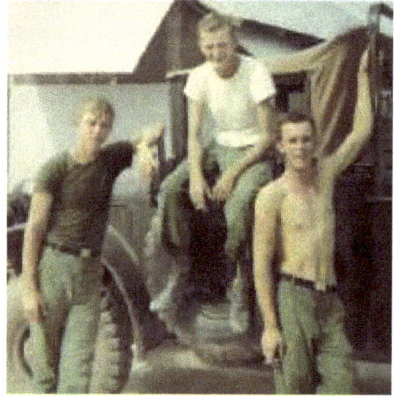

Dick Long, George Tripp,
Reb Pearson, Phu Bai, 1968

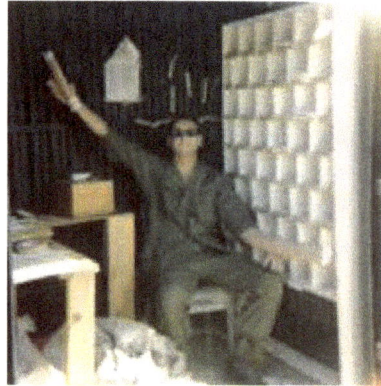

"The Avdul", Donald.
Mail Call, Phu Bai, 1969

Bobby Walker and Pete Leonard
checking the gear

Bravery shines when under fire
Courage when the task is dire
But tough, hard work in every way
Got us through each brutal day.

Blast Bunker, Phu Bai, 1968,
(water down below)

Vince Cedola, dishin' the
dirt, leading by example

The commonplace, round the clock, 24/7 cycle of cooperation, dedication, expertise and effort it took to stand our ground in Vietnam was relentless. Each man had a part and when one part of the machine broke down, men died.

On an average day, a nothing much happened day, an interlude of blissful quiet, the unyielding effort still was necessary, demanding, straining. THERE.

NINETY ONE BRAVO

The medics, can't think where to start,
To describe their courage, describe their heart,
Their only task at war each day,
To save a life, hold death at bay.

Into combat they would shun,
The false protection of a gun,
They held instead their medic's gear,
And faced the carnage without fear.

What fear they had they put aside,
To tend the wounded, stay by their side,
To give them comfort, shed a tear,
To hold their hand when death was near.

44th Medical Brigade
Patches, Combat Medics
Badge

Dustoff medics, our own rare breed,
Rose up above that noble creed,
To tend the shattered in the air,
To see them safe to doctor's care.

They stopped the bleeding, helped them breathe,
Cleaned their wounds, watched them grieve,
They knelt beside them on the flight,
With care and prayer, with all their might,
That they would see them safely where,
The hospitals could do their share.

And when the wounded left their ship,
Bandaged tight on morphine's drip,
They washed their hands, these medic men
And turned to do it all again.

Nine One Bravo, none more brave
Whose only task a life to save,
And still and all nowhere to start
To describe their courage, to describe their heart.

Harry Geist, Medic,
Phu Bai, 1968

Bob Byrd, Medic, Phu Bai,
1968, Wounded in Action

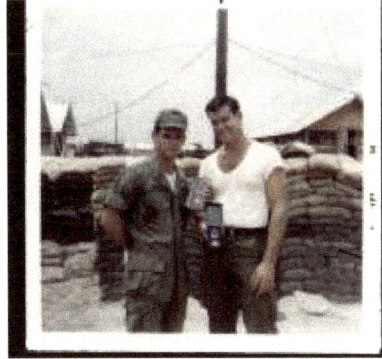

Gene Fisher, Flyboy,
Willie Skoal, Medic,
Phu Bai, 1968

Steve Cogliano, Crew
Chief, Phu Bai, 1968,
Wounded in Action

Try to imagine how insignificant it feels to whine about my tasks, to chronicle my laments and heart sickness at what surrounded me when I think about what our medics, all medics, went through. All the dirt, sweat, heartache and misery PLUS the responsibility of lives passing through their hands on the way to trained physicians.

Kids, again the most remarkable aspect. I do not recall a single medic in our unit in all the time I was there who was older than, maybe, 25.

Two rapid fire months at Fort Sam Houston Texas to learn the basics, then up to their hips and eyeballs in catastrophic, horrific injuries. Blasts, and burns and jagged holes packed in mud and miles from help.

We asked a lot from the medics. They delivered.

TRIAGE

With the wounded in our ship
Bandaged for the hospital trip
We came to learn to watch their eyes
For in them pain had no disguise.

Some in shock, eyes wide with fear,
Or eyes closed tight as death drew near,
Cries for help that made no sound,
Silent eyes more lost than found.

Eyes that saw things far away,
Eyes not to see another day,
Wounded men now in our charge
With hurts that were so very large.

Battered, bruised, mutilated,
Burned, bashed, asphyxiated,
Every kind of human broken,
In our care where mercy's spoken.

Clear the airway, stop the bleeding,
Give them what they most were needing,
A friendly pat, a quick, brave smile,
To help them hold on for a while.

Don't give if a sign when wounds looked bad,
We were the hope they haven't had,
Tell them that they'd be okay,
Help them breathe, help them pray.

As our ship sped across the sky
To get them care before they'd die,
We all knew we were in a race
To not stare death dead in the face.

Most survived, that's a fact,
Our medics knew just how to act,
We'd get them where they would find rest
After treatment from our very best

Again, the Medics. I'm still in awe. I scrambled across many a helicopter deck to hold a bandage, apply pressure, lend a hand, always terrified at how far out of my element I was. I followed the medic's instructions, tried to stay calm, tried to keep the look of horror off my face. We all did.

"*a special word about the 'Dust Offs'* —
the medevacs...

COURAGE ABOVE AND BEYOND THE CALL OF DUTY WAS SORT OF ROUTINE TO THEM. IT WAS A DAILY THING, PART OF THE WAY THEY LIVED. THAT'S THE GREAT PART AND IT MEANT SO MUCH TO EVERY LAST MAN WHO SERVED THERE.

WHETHER HE EVER GOT HURT OR NOT, HE KNEW 'DUST OFF' WAS THERE.

IT WAS A GREAT THING FOR OUR PEOPLE."

General Creighton W. Abrams
Chief of Staff
United States Army

WHITE SHIPS NEARBY
(Everything is Grace)

REPOSE, REPOSE shining bright,
Off the coastline in the night,
Glows like heaven's sacred light,
To guide our ships, to soothe our sight.
Safe haven from the jungle fight.

Ship of Kindness, Ship of Care,
Our wounded would find refuge there,
You took them in, you eased their hurt
You washed away their blood and dirt.
Cool, clean beds below your decks,
Human beings from human wrecks.

USS Sanctuary,
South China Sea,
Coast of Vietnam

In blue pajamas wrapped in smiles,
You readied them for homeward miles,
You gave them comfort, gave them ease,
And rescued them from war's disease.
Their dues all paid, their mission through
As we passed them from us to you.

USS Repose, South China
Sea, Coast of Vietnam

SANCTUARY, SANCTUARY, sister ship,
Same-same REPOSE on Mercy's trip,
Shining brightly off the shore,
As wounded mounted by the score.

SANCTUARY'S noble crew,
Did all the same REPOSE would do.
For their star shining through the night
Was ever clear and ever bright.

Two ships of white and all aglow,
Gave us hope and let us know
In all the world gone up in flames,
REPOSE, SANCTUARY, sacred names,
Ships of kindness, ships of care,
Our world was better with you there.

Dustoff Aboard USS
Repose, South China
Sea, 1969

The Author and Vince
Cedola aboard USS Repose,
South China Sea, 1968

Ken Hogan, Vince Cedola,
Will Skoal, Len Gann
aboard USS Sanctuary,
1968

Real deal. Nothing in Fantasyland, Tinsel town, or Never-Ever Land could match
the magic of these ships. Doctors, nurses, crew, clean sheets, coffee, sandwiches,
safe refuge, serenity, a blessed island floating nearby.

ANGELS IN THEIR EYES
(Who Knew?)

That's me with the goofy grin,
Leaning on a pole,
Those other guys, they're smiling too,
Says something 'bout our role.

We're all here in bad ol' Nam,
A very nasty place,
But look at us, this grinning lot,
A smile on every face.

Ray Barnett, Henry Birchall, the Author, Phu Bai, 1968

Angels in those eyes I see,
Looking backward through the years,
Angels in our eyes because,
In spite of all our fears,
Our job, our task, our daily duty,
Was saving lives, a thing of beauty.

No matter what each role we'd play,
We all served mercy's task,
Never a man to shirk the job,
All you had to do was ask.

We stayed the course and played our part,
Rose above war's grim lies,
We kept our faith among ourselves
And gained Angels in our eyes.

Don Avdul, Phil Rugen, Phu Bai, 1969

Larry Woodyard, Phu Bai, 1969

Despite the madness, the brutality, the terminal suffering, despair and heartache our unit was blessed with the redeeming grace of our mission. I saw guys frightened, I saw them cry, bitch, moan, complain, and suffer, but I never, ever saw them falter in their job, our job, TO SAVE A LIFE.

DEROS
(Date Estimated Return From Overseas)

A magical word
With a magical date
For as we faced our hidden fate
The only magic in our world
Was DEROS.

A backward count from 365
Make the count, we stay alive.
But should we stumble along the way,
We'd never get to DEROS day.

A ticking bomb, a burning fuse,
A distant day to win or lose.
Always in sight, but never near,
Our fondest hope, our greatest fear,

And when our DEROS finally came,
Just as we felt we'd won the game,
We'd leave our pals, leave our mates,
To hurry home for high school dates,

We'd drive fast cars, drink some beer
Forget about our whole Nam year.
Just get me home. I'll be okay,
I'll think of Nam some other day.

That wouldn't work we didn't know,
There was no ending to this show,
Only then we understood,
How bittersweet was DEROS.

Nothing meant more than going home, NOTHING. I knew how much I had changed, I hoped, I prayed, that going home was going to restore me to the old me. There really wasn't much time to think the process through, it was business enough not thinking about what was going on in the present to delve too deeply into the uncertain reality of the future. DEROS was a fantasy. I desperately needed a fantasy.

ONE MORE TIME

This one's hard so listen tight,
I'm still not sure I explain it right,
When my tour ended after a year
I decided to stay over here.

DEROS dates, Stateside schemes,
Didn't mean all that much it seems,
Even knowing I survived
Didn't matter when my day arrived.

Six months more I signed up for,
And after that a few months more,
I'd stay in country with my mates,
And get me some new DEROS dates.

So I stayed on I volunteered,
To my family's shock and woe,
They wanted me back home and safe,
And often told me so.

The reason why's the hardest part,
The answer lies within my heart,
In a world where there was so much bad
The Dustoff team was all I had.

The goodness here, the mercy flight,
The sense of doing something right,
Being part of such a team,
Holding firm to compassion's dream.

Serving where it mattered most,
Standing fast at danger's post,
Being in a unit where,
I learned how deeply I could care.

I wasn't done, I had to share
The skills I learned by being where,
Staying strong and being true
Counted most in what I'd do.

All that's true it's genuine,
And very much worth knowing
But truth be told, inside I felt
I wasn't finished growing.

In Asia's soil, in combat's air,
I learned to be a man
Meant doing more than just your part,
It meant doing all you can.

I knew I hadn't reached my all,
There was more that I could give
And doing what I'd learned to do
Meant more wounded just might live.

So marching on I passed up my ride
On the magic Freedom Bird,
I stayed in place, to live in Grace,
And live up to my word.

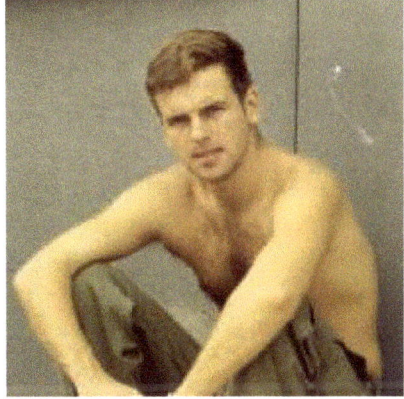

The Author, Phu Bai, 1968

That is as close as I can come to understanding why I stayed. In Today's world my long ago reasons seem corny, naïve, foolish, but not there, not then.

Perhaps the world has lost too much corny, too much naiveté, it most certainly has lost too much dedication, too much altruism, too much of why I, and a lot of men like me, chose to stay beyond our first tour in Vietnam.

1969 IN COUNTRY

The ass end of the sixties,
Another year of war,
Not a lot to write about,
'Cept what all the killings for.

The total tab, US, this year,
Eleven Thousand Plus,
A thousand men a month damn near,
From those here among us.

It's all about the dead men now,
No talk of victory,
Kill more of them, than they kill us,
Is all there seems to be.

The war grinds on,
Day in, day out,
Time passes very slow,
What terrified me yesterday,
Today I hardly know.

My Lai lies in ashes,
The A-Shau's like the moon,
There's blood on every paddy dike,
Lunch is served at noon.

The hospitals are all stuffed full,
There's wounded everywhere,
Sometimes we watch a movie,
Sometimes we sit and stare.

The smoke, the fire, the big guns boom,
That acrid gunfire smell,
Goes on and on, day and night,
Like daydreaming in hell.

Back home there's all these rumors,
'Bout winding down the fight,
Meanwhile a thousand guys a month
Are dying left and right.

If I can make it through this year
Until my orders come,
I'll walk away and try to make
Some sense of what we've done.

Till then I'll push my fears away
And do my duty day to day,
To Save A Life my unit's creed
A commitment I so badly need.

I'll soldier on, I know the drill,
Thank God our mission shines,
Inside my head grave questions twist
And strangle me like vines.

1969, the last year of my tour,
I've counted each and every day,
You know, just to be sure,

I hope that I'm still standing
When they show me to the door,
Because there's not enough inside of me,
To stay here one day more.

Darkness now, hope for victory is gone forever, searching for the point, wondering how the war will end and why it is still going on. Lots of shifty-eyed politicians popping up, double talking the truth which is lost in smoke and fire.

1969 THE WORLD

Back home, another time and place
With Nixon now the nation's face,
Peaceniks tasting lots of mace
And meanwhile, out in space, a race.

Neil and Buzz walk on the moon,
Butch and Sundance make lady's swoon,
Broadway Joe earns football fame,
A Cleveland river bursts into flame.

Woodstock looks like lots of fun.
With lots of rain and little sun,
Peace, love, dope, still on the rise,
As hippies sport their false disguise.

Manson's creepy family
Gets lots of coverage on TV
While ratings for the Asian war
Are falling right down through the floor.

Veteran's graveyards getting full,
Politician's constant bull,
The polls they're taking clearly say,
They want this war to go away.

Perhaps this year back home they'll hear,
What we could whisper in their ear,
More soldiers coming home in bags
Does little good once commitment sags.

The time is now for them to act,
Turn down the music, face the fact,
This war is lost, there's no denying,
Or lots more mothers will be crying.
'69 end of an age,

Time to turn the decade's page
Forget what we've been fighting for
And end this bloody Asian war.

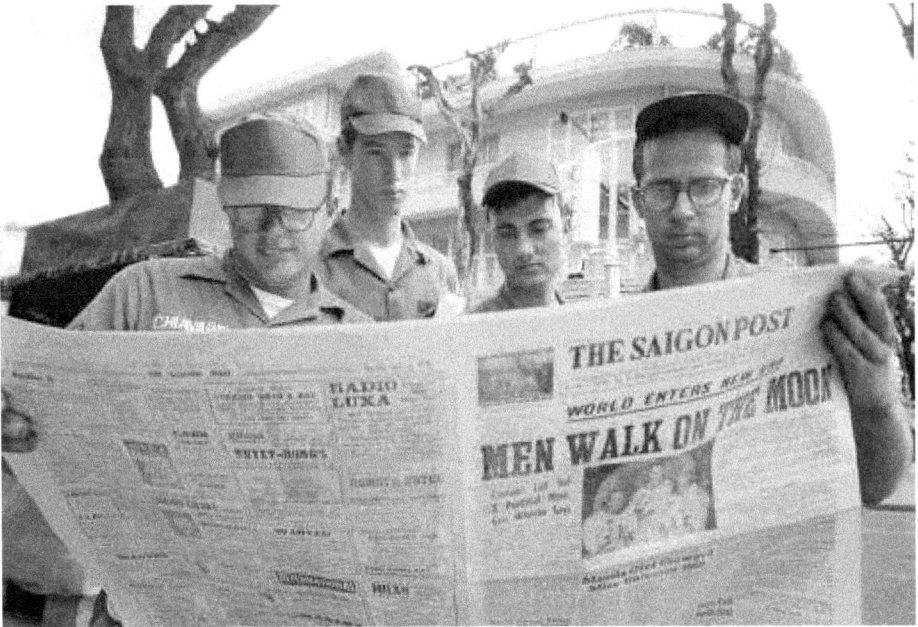

A faraway place, back home, the world. Super Bowls and Rock concerts, moon walks, press conferences, all seemed so trivial, so insignificant from where we stood, next to what we were doing. It was like watching a beach party from inside a live volcano.

FNG'S
(Ours)

Fresh New Guys, that's the tag,
If delicate you be
But usually a big F-bomb
Went before the N and G.

But any way you said it
They were all brand new
New to Nam, new to war
And new to what to do.

Our replacements were arriving,
The men who'd take our place,
As full of noise as Cherry Boys,
The kind we used to be.

They're dangerous to be around
All us old guys said,
They don't know all the ins and outs
And will probably end up dead.

They better learn to play this game
And follow all the rules,
Failure here's a lot more harsh
Then back in Stateside schools.

They latch onto us old guys
And smile when we say boo,

They'll only learn to stay alive
By doing what we do.

As days go on, eyes open wide,
They're learning all the ropes,
Pay attention, don't ask why,
Try not to act like dopes.

Takes about a month I guess,
Maybe a little more,
To stop feeling like they're on the moon,
To know what is in store.

The brutal facts, the final score,
There was no nine to five,
24/7 on alert,
If they want to stay alive.

Trust your buddy, load your gun,
Watch the native folk,
Someone's gonna pay the price,
And that is not a joke.

FNG, the new guy tag,
Eventually had its day
But not before their Stateside schemes
Like ours had drained away.

These next guys in, replacing us,
Would face our grim routine,
The war's still needing lots of men
To feed the Death Machine.

So when it was our turn to teach
New Dustoff's to behave,
We'd did it fine without the con,
'Cause Lives is what we save.

The flip side of Cherry Boys. I know we treated our own better than many were received, had to, we had a job to do.

BODY COUNT
(What The Hell?)

A whole new way of keeping score,
Of who would win this crazy War,
10 of them, 2 of US,
No need for making such a fuss.

On TV, the General's grinning,
10 to 2, we must be winning.
Never really saw those 10,
But on the scoreboard they were men.

Now our 2, yeah, they had real names,
And hopes and dreams and lover's flames,
Though they don't have them anymore,
They're just a part of this week's score.

Body Count, tote up the dead,
To show we're winning, we're ahead,
Funny way to run a war,
Are numbers all we're fighting for?

If they were 2 and we were 10,
Could we call it off, go home again?
I just don't get this, count a head,
How does it end, when we're all dead?

The insanity of it all, the hypocrisy, the lies hit their peak around this time. What we saw every day had very little to do with the way the war was being reported.

NIGHT HOIST MISSION
(No Kiddin')

An urgent call from in the night,
For dying wounded and,
They're beneath the jungle canopy
With no place we can land.

This one's drenched in danger
There is no doubt at all
Night hoist above the jungle
The deadliest of all.

Now med-evacs from hot LZ's
We had a simple plan,
Go in fast, get out quick
And never leave a man.

But when the wounded gathered where
We couldn't land our ship,
We took a hoist and pulled them up,
A very different trip.

A hoist is like a fishing pole,
With a basket at the base,
We'd lower it through the jungle
To bring the wounded from that place.

The fear we never spoke about
Kept locked down deep inside
Raced through our blood all icy cold
On every hoist trip ride.

The crew, locked in, each one of us
Vital purpose in our eyes
One wrong move, one small mistake,
And everybody dies.

We kept the chatter turned down low
Grim purpose on this flight,
To hover steady in the sky,
Biggest target in the night.

Our ship held still, the lifeline down,
No swaying in the breeze,
The slightest movement of the ship
Crushed wounded in the trees.

A slow trip down, a slow trip up,
And knowing all the while
The enemy was all around
They could see us for a mile.

Once we got the wounded in
And stowed our dangling gear
We broke away and got up high
Trading altitude for fear.

Night hoists in the jungle
A not uncommon chore
But each and every one for us
The most frightening of the war.

On the Hoist (dangling target)

Nothing here but the personal certainty that this could be it, blown out of the sky, falling, burning in the trees, death come out of nowhere.

I recall finding my hands clenched into fists around my weapon and I couldn't, at first, unclench my fingers. Breathing in, breathing out, don't think, behave as trained, watch your buddies. Hold on tight.

MAIL CALL
(Incoming)

I never felt so far away
As when your letter came today,
Miles and miles and more apart,
It choked my throat, it broke my heart.

Your letter full of howdy-do,
Our teams on fire and how are you?
I read it on a sand-bagged wall,
When rockets come, that's where we crawl.

I set aside my fresh cleaned gun,
While you told me all about the fun
Of circus rides and sandy beaches,
I scratched my leg to check for leeches.

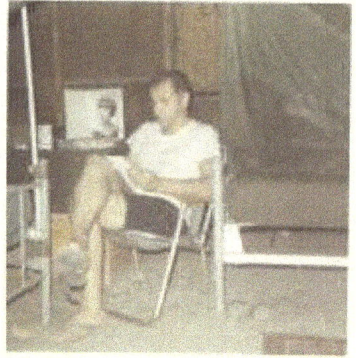

Don Avdul, The hooch,
Phu Bai, 1968

With every word you'd written down,
I missed my home, I missed my town,
I missed you too, the most right then,
I fell apart, inside, till when,
I pulled myself together back,
In case the enemy did attack,

As I read on of all your news,
Inside me rose those deadly blues,
I suck in air, I check my post,
Here vigilance is what matters most,
No more for me the tender phrase,
My guard stays up, my life a daze.

You had to go, your letter said,
I have to stay among the dead.
For I'm not the me that you recall,
I've changed, I strain to feel at all,
So much the better on this hill,
If death don't take me, sadness will.

Please write again, I need to know,
That someone, somewhere here below
Can give me hope, that after all,
I can make it till the next mail call.

The Author, Phu Bai, 1968

The change has set, I hardly remember who I used to be. I'm not a kid anymore, I'm not an adult, I'm not sure I want to know what I am. The important thing, to me, is hiding the change.

R & R
(Rest and Relaxation?)

R&R, one week away,
A safer place to rest and play,
Sydney, Bangkok or Hong Kong,
Party hearty, smoke a bong.

Live it up in a plush hotel,
The girls are cheap,
The drinks are swell,
Got to sleep without a gun,
Got real drunk and called it fun.

In Singapore, Penang, Tapei,
This is what we'd do all day,
From topless bars to boom-boom joint,
We behaved like trash,
And that's the point.

We were your kids, on leave from war,
Didn't we deserve a little more?
Manila, Tokyo, Singapore,
Hit the town, Git a whore.

I wish I'd known a better way
To spend my precious time away,
Not much here to write the folks,
Drip, drip clap and dirty jokes.

R&R, a week long gone,
We had a blast, a Fuck-a-Thon,
Lots of booze and whores and dope,
Though little there to give us hope,
We'd rise from this as better men,
On R&R I failed again.

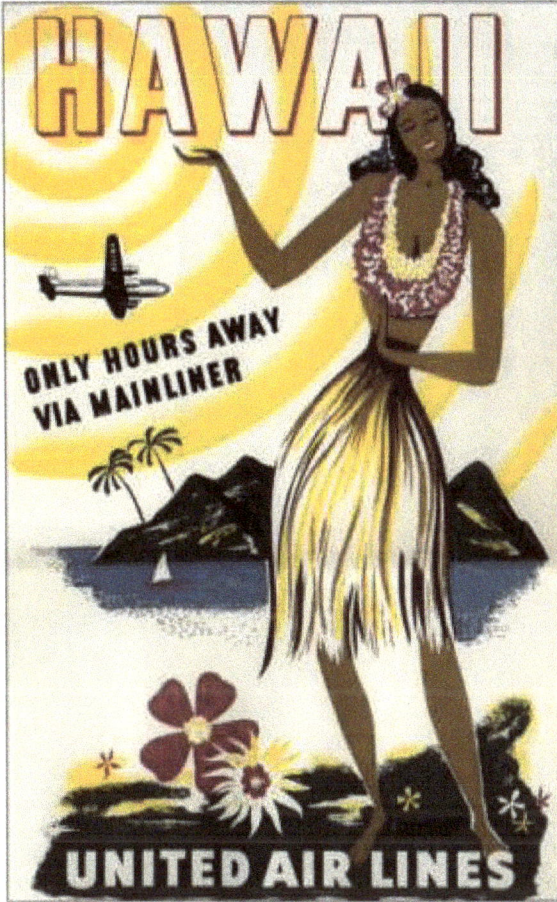

It seems unmanly to question the trip, the process the hearty party. Booze, whores, dope, very hazy limits. This is not how I was raised, nor taught to behave, but I did all the low down, sleazy, dishonorable things. Did them, bragged about them, though had I been a little older, a lot wiser, I might have been ashamed.

You'd think that whoever was running this program could have done a little better. Did they think so little of us as human beings that this was the way they expected us to behave? I wasn't PERSON enough to make better choices for myself yet. I went along, did the deed, leered my lecher smile, another experience I had to keep secret from the decent folk.

DEAR JOHN

Is what the letter said,
The one that soldiers most did dread,
Didn't matter what's your name,
Heartbreak was this letter's game.

There's someone new the girl would write,
And how's your little jungle fight?
I won't be writing any more,
You filthy bitch, you dirty whore!

At least those were the words to scream
As tears eroded all your dreams,
It happened like they said it would
Jody's there, and that ain't good.

I never took this kind of hit,
I couldn't handle that kind of shit,
I'd broken off the girlfriend game
Long before a letter came.

But those who didn't, took the dare
This letter wouldn't find them where
There was no place to sit and cry,
There was no time to wonder why.

Can't be walking round these parts
With crying eyes or broken hearts,
Romance is for another day
Best to live the Army way.

Do your duty, keep up your guard,
Clean your weapon, drink real hard,
Never show your softer side,
Don't get taken for a ride.

Letters starting out "Dear John",
Always sends this message on,
Keep your heart where it won't bust,
Be very careful who you trust.

Don't make many friends that way,
But those you make will never say,
I won't be writing any more,
You dirty bitch, you filthy whore!

Anger, rage, hellfire and damnation, these were our constant, safe, permissible emotions. They smothered fear, drowned pity and buried, briefly, our inner hurts.

These letters were like gunshots from back home. Deadly, like friendly fire, grave wounded, the body goes on, the spirit dies. Hope, memories, even the fantasy sort, were so vital to us then that having them disappear decreased the motivation to fight the anguish, brutality and senselessness of what we saw around us. I was still too young to embrace the whole true love thing, but if never looked more dangerous, even lethal, than when a friend got one of these letters.

WALKOUT
(Sayonara)

The day has come,
His not yours,
As buddies reach the end of tours.

We'd walk then out,
On their way home,
And wonder how we'd go on alone.

They'd pack their bags with giant smiles,
Our hearts go with them,
Mile by mile.

We'd check their bunks,
An empty space,
And yearn for their familiar face,
Unspoken words, the buddies touch,
Each one to miss, so very much.

The very instant they were gone,
A new face came,
Wide eyed, forlorn.

He'd try to be the buddy lost,
But couldn't melt our heart's safe frost.
"Cause one day when our time to go,
Had us leave behind each man we'd know,
We'd look ahead, act unafraid,
Then walkout for our farewell parade.

As one by one we'd take our leave,
A freedom bird on which to grieve
Sight unseen for departed friends,
Walkout's when our communion ends.

Friends leave. Friends die. Friends get wounded. Friends disappear. The cost keeps going up. It's insane. And people wonder why we are shut down.

LAST LOOK AROUND
(October, 1969)

My walkout now, my turn to go,
Enlistment up, end of show,
Left my rifle, left my bunk,
Left a great big pile of junk.

I'm going home, I should not feel sad,
If I felt at all I might be glad,
Not sure what I'm supposed to feel,
This going home's a scary deal.

Best to take this very slow,
And stick with things I'd come to know,
Keep my chin up, don't let on,
Smile and wave and just get gone.

With Danny H my hooch mate friend
Who waited for my tour to end
So we'd fly home as pals together,
To face the Stateside Autumn weather.

The guys we're leaving all are nice,
With yearning in their eyes,
Their longing to walk out with us
A very frail disguise.

With smoke on skids, they flew us out
Skimmed low across the pad,
Our last goodbye, a fond salute.
The best I'd ever had.

As Phu Bai faded in my past
And civilian life did beckon,
The part of me I'd leave behind
Was more than I could reckon.

In two quick days this all would be
A withered dream, a memory,
A tale that only I would know
At least right then I sure hoped so.

I recall the experience as like trying to watch two, even three movies at the same time, farewell to friends, longing to be home, worried about what happens next, hoping everything was going to be a whole lot better than it inevitably ever could be.

Danny H is my Good Guy buddy, Danny Hidalgo, "Supply".

FREEDOM BIRD

Silver airplane, shiny bright,
On the runway bathed in light,
Door wide open, stairway down
My golden ticket out of town.

Across the tarmac we march in
Upon each face a giant grin,
Look around, find a seat
Feel my heart's astounding beat.

Things settle down, the door is locked,
Engines roar, the wheels unblocked,
Down the runway roaring fast,
And then, the thrill, airborne at last,

A joyous sound escapes my soul,
I'm still alive, my hallowed goal,
The guys around me laugh and smile,
I catch my breath, which takes a while.

A girl in blue, a jaunty hat,
Welcomes us aboard, and tells us that,
The drinks are free, they'll serve a meal,
The flight is long, this dream's for real.

Out the window, one last look,
Safe at last, inside I shook,
I said goodbye to Nam but she
Would never say goodbye to me.

Crystal clear, unforgettable, imprecise.

BACK IN THE WORLD

My orders came, my tour is through
I'm going home, I'm overdue,
One more year on Nam's green shores
And firefights and boom-boom whores,
I'd never go, I'd have to stay
And live my life the Asian way.

I'm getting out, no time to spare,
I'm awfully used to living there,
Take my word, I need out quick,
And going home is just the trick.

So on the plane with a great big smile,
But inside I'm thinking, wait a while,
Let's take this slow, please understand,
I'm not quite fit for Disneyland.

Got some rough ways, a dirty tongue,
I eat real fast, I don't act young,
It's hard to laugh and when I smile,
It hides my feelings for a while.

All that said you shipped me through,
Paid me off and said skidoo,
I'm on my own back in the States,
Land of Dreams and Golden Gates.

So now I'm here, I look around,
At all the sights and all the sounds,
Squeaky clean and shiny bright,
And no one ready for the fight.

You talk too loud, stand in the clear,
At night you don't see danger near,
You don't seem rough, you don't seem steady,
And I am always, always, ready.

I pack a gun and screw the law,
It keeps me safe from what I saw,
I don't sleep deep, I'm half awake,
An hour or two is all I take.

Where's the sentries? Where's the guards?
No sandbags round your house and yards,
Your streets too bright, can't see the flare,
And Charlie could be anywhere.

I hang around and hear you chatter
'bout lots of stuff that doesn't matter,
Sports or movies, or TV,
Rock stars, fast cars, calories.
You all sound like a bunch of dopes,
Can this be where I hung my hopes?

I can't say all this stuff out loud,
I'd get locked up by your tame crowd,
I very wired, very tight,
And it gets worse around twilight,
As night draws near I lock and load,
The softest sound, I might explode.

Back in Nam I knew my place,
My life had purpose, I lived in Grace,
I pledged MY LIFE if had to be,
To save that country's liberty,
Your cause, not mine, when I went there,
Till war taught me how to care.

So on those nights when I can dream,
I dream about my Phu Bai team,
Ready there in fading light,
For a cry for mercy in the night.

I can't go back, I see that clear,
My war is lost, no victory near,
Though my friends fight on and brave the sky,
In valor's name prepared to die,
From in the world I see it plain,
Nobody cares, it's all in vain.

Here in the world I'll live out my days,
Watching all the Stateside plays,
But in my heart this secret stays,
I was better off with Asian ways.

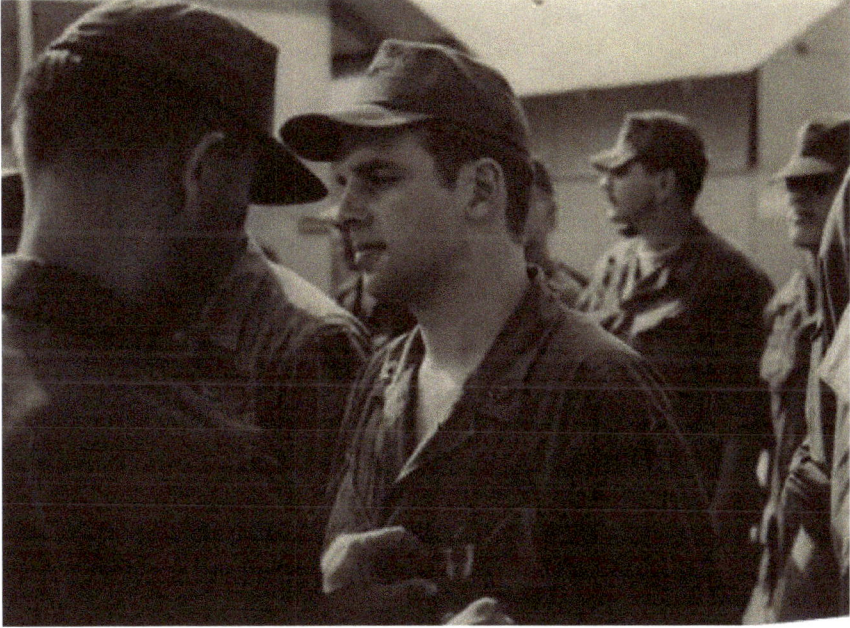

The Author, Award Ceremony, Phu Bai, 1968

Back through the looking glass, THE WORLD now felt like the moon. Nam was comprehensible, an established habit. I missed it more each day. Others have said this better, but this is pretty much how it was for me. I've left out much of my anger, resentment, my extreme feelings of rejection, they were easy to wallow in, but underneath all that, it hurt.

ASIAN DREAMS
(The Middle Years)

Diggin' ditches, buying stuff,
Movin' round, playing tough,
Dancing slow and dancing fast,
Nothing good that seems to last.

Spending money, wasting time,
Trying to get my life to rhyme.
Pack the car, hit the road,
Wishing someone could share the load.

Buy some jewelry, buy a house,
Say "I DO", become a louse,
Start again without a clue,
To find the right thing I can do.

Keeping score by making money,
Pretending life is always sunny,
Looking for a cause that's just,
Getting older, fighting rust.

Looking out for only me,
Trying to find out who to be,
Find a hobby, take a class,
As life just kinda' kicks my ass.

Don't know where to put the blame,
To give my emptiness a name,
Not the way I set out to be,
Can't figure out what's wrong with me.

I miss my good old Army days,
But that's a secret that never pays,
I miss the goals we common shared,
I miss how much I really cared.

I guess whatever path I find,
Will have to come from my own mind,
Civilian life ain't all it seems,
And I can't shake my Asian dreams.

Time stacks up, years roll by, good times and bad. Trying to keep my
successes ahead of my regrets.

From left kneeling, Steve Cox, Albert
Witschen, the Author. **Rear**, Gary Shepherd,
Johnnie Kirk, Danny Hidalgo

From left, Roger Yost, unknown, the Author, James
Adair, Vince Cedola

POPPA TANGO SIERRA DELTA
(The Breakdown)

After years of getting by,
And keeping secrets on the sly,
Sleeping nights 'bout half awake,
Hiding how my heart did ache,
Finally done with how I think,
I made a date to see a shrink.

It's not easy letting go,
And letting other people know,
I need some help, I can't get by,
No matter how hard that I try.
The past they say is far away,
The past is with me every day.

So in I went and hunkered down,
In case this guy's another clown,
Who'll tell me what he thinks I think,
And waits for me to finally blink.

I suppose he's talkin' 'bout what he knows,
From in some book or school house show,
He sounds real sure he can't be wrong,
But to me it's still the same old song:

"Love Your neighbor,
Lend a hand,
Obey the rules,
Know where you stand,
Don't get angry, blow a fuse,
Be careful of the drugs you use."

Sound advice but not for me,
I've bigger fish to fry you see.
KIA's and body bags,
Broken men and bloody rags.

And at that point we drift apart,
He can't imagine what's in my heart,
So out the door once more I go,
Not knowing what I need to know.

More years go by,
I'm faking stable,
And then one day they find a label,
A way to sum up what's wrong with me,
In short, it's called PTSD.

Post-Traumatic Stress Disorder,
Quite a mouthful, quite and order,
They talked to lots and lots of vets,
And on those words they hung their bets.

After combat, after trauma,
After any major drama,
Some people tend to fall apart,
While others soldier on, to start,
And then one day they too break down,
And join the others on the ground.

Always jumpy, always wary,
Looking out for what is scary,
Can't enjoy civilian fun,
Hiding out my secret gun,
All of these they say will be
A sign I have PTSD.

Frozen feelings, forever blue,
Daily sadness, without a clue,
Isolation, by myself,
Poison pills on a hidden shelf.

My rage is doing very well,
The slightest tick, my heads in hell.
Can't describe the way I feel,
Love can't get past my heart of steel.
Symptom clusters so they say
For veterans who earned combat pay.

I tell them, then they tell me,
Seems I've got PTSD,
The words, they hit me like a gun,
I thought I was the only one.

Yeah, that's me, my secrets through,
They've found me out, I know it's true,
They tell me what they think I need,
And watch me cry, that's how I bleed.

About the cure, it's sad to say,
The cure is for another day,
Meanwhile they've got lots of drugs,
And yellow ribbons, lots of hugs.

They toss us disability bucks,
The more we get, the less it sucks,
But still we've got one thing to say;
And shout it each and every day,
Do what's right, stop the flow.
Of sending soldiers where you know,
The braver that they try to be,
The worse they'll get PTSD.

Poppa Tango Sierra Delta,
The hidden wound, the secret shelter,
A label pasted over me,
And soldiers through eternity.

The Author, far right with the Vets
Anaheim Vet Center
1982

Yeah, I blinked. Making my problems clear didn't necessarily make them better. Understanding is only part of the cure. Good intentions don't necessarily produce good results.

The symptoms are accurate, the definition is certain and there is definitely some relief in knowing I do not suffer alone, but what to do? Life goes on, as apparently does therapy, till the end.

VENUS IMPACTED
(All The Fair Young Maidens)

Wives and Girlfriends are and ain't
Most they have the same complaint,
Sometimes I'm here,
Sometimes I'm not.
And blame it on the war I fought,
Many years and long ago,
Still in my heart, like frozen snow.

When they get mad and start to curse,
I shut down and make it worse,
What's left is that I'm never right,
Up until the next heart fight.

What they don't get is their arrival,
Complicates my own survival,
Makes my life much harder when,
I can't explain my inner Zen
So every tiff I lose you see,
'Cause they can quote PTSD,
I have it bad in every way,
At least that's what the experts say.

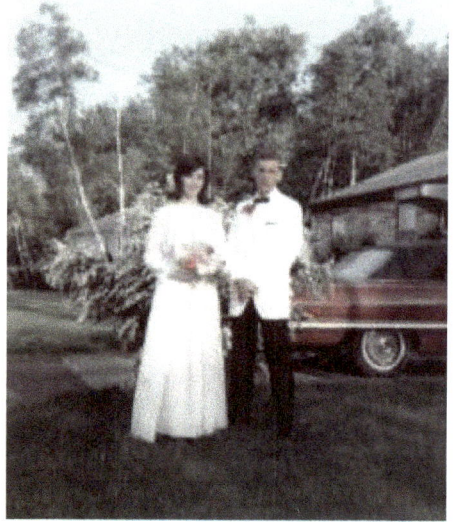

The Author, Senior Prom,
Lowell, MA 1965

But they don't live inside my head,
Or lay with me upon my bed.
The hearts and flowers game I guess,
I'll never win and I'll confess,
Perhaps it's best I don't play at all,
But when I don't my world gets small.

As all around me things do shrink,
I'm only left with what I think,
A chain of thought that will never be,
Free of good old PTSD.

Wives and Girlfriends bless their hearts,
Them that don't take off for better parts,
But stick around and stay the course,
And don't just leave us in divorce,
Will always have our gratitude,
Though hidden 'neath our attitude,
For love comes hard, and seldom spoken,
For those of us the war had broken.

They are and ain't

Miles of Rocky Road here. It took me a long time to figure out broken people seek out broken people and two wrongs rarely make a right.

BELEAGURED ROOFTOP, HELICOPTER HOVERING, REFUGEES CLINGING TO THE SKIDS, PANICKED MASSES, SMOKE ON THE HORIZON, FIRE IN THE TREES. JUDGEMENT DAY HAS COME TO SAIGON, APRIL 30, 1975.

I watched it happen on TV,
Flickering images of "How can this be?"
All for nothing our buddies bled,
60,000 U.S. dead.

The South collapses, newsmen speak,
North to South in under a week,
Wringing hands and standing down,
The Generals are all out of town.

White House Silent, Pentagon mute,
As Vietnam goes down the chute,
All the war birds will not fly,
The Pacific Fleet just standing by.

Now we're running,
No other way,
To spin this tale,
To blur this day.

From the rooftops people screaming,
Loaded, one last chopper leaving,
Now we've left them to their fate,
To an enemy filled with hate.

No uniforms among this crowd,
They'd got out before the guns got loud,
And left behind this hopeless crew,
Who took our word that we'd be true.

Saigon Rooftop, April 30, 1975

Without warning I felt my tears,
As memories crashed down through the years,
Brave men dying, the wounded's cries,
All the promises, all the lies.

I turned away and hid my face,
From crying in a public place,
I watched the people walking by,
As Saigon died their eyes were dry.

Don't you care? I yearned to shout,
We lost this war, the secret's out,
That we won't honor what we pledge,
That we're no longer freedom's edge.

Our flag which never knew defeat
Is burning in a Saigon street,
I felt that it was I alone,
Who cared, or who had even known,
We gave our word that they'd be free,
And now we broke it, on TV.

April 30, 1975.
For those we left behind,
Freedom will never be…

Some of the most horrific images still in my head come from this day. Helicopters pushed into the ocean, our flag being dragged behind an NVA tank, terrified people we abandoned, waste. The war hardened my heart, this day broke my heart.

CHOSEN MEN

**The Vietnam Veteran's Memorial,
November, 1982**

*They told us that they loved us,
Were behind us all the way,
Baby killers, pot heads,
The ones that couldn't get away.*

*We were the nations finest,
The bravest in the land,
Fools and dupes and suckers,
Mindless killers for The Man.*

*We pledged allegiance to the flag,
Our nation and each other,
We got kicked out of the family
By our sisters and our brothers.*

*Victory or death they said,
And we who did not die,
But soldiered on from dawn to dawn,
We caught them in their lie.*

*You lost the war! They'd yell and scream
And damn us for their failure
To see that we had pledged our lives
To be a nation's savior.*

*They never tied a ribbon
Round our old oaken tree,
Just told us to be quiet,
They'd forgiven us, you see.*

*They told us that they loved us,
We were the best of all,*
***But they only gave a nation's love
To those there on our Wall.***

Photograph by
Dennis (Frenchy) Troule

Things got better as the years rolled on. Lots of anguish in between the better and the bad. Besides, we heard you the first time.

CIVILIANS
National Anthem, Fenway Park, September 10, 1996

Should they know the fight at Ia Drang?
We lost three hundred dead,
Or digging deep on Khe Sanh's hills,
Surrounded as they bled?

From Saigon's fall to Imperial Hue,
Forgotten fights in our safe day,
An Loc's stand, Ben Het's Berets,
Quang Tri's siege, Tet's worst days.

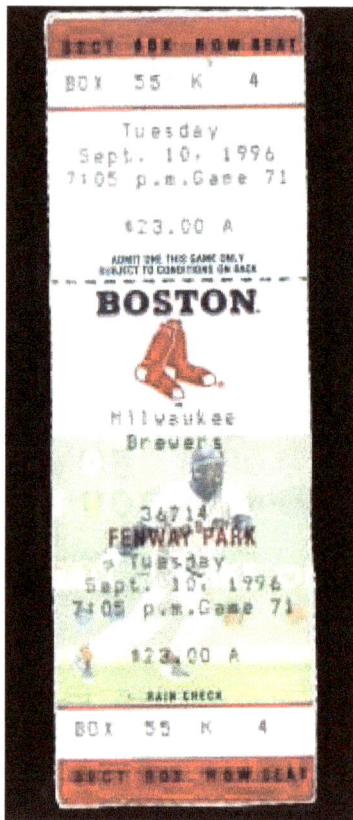

Dewey Canyon's brave Marines,
Junction City's jungle scenes,
Con Tien and Allen Brook,
Go Noi Island, ground we took.

Hamburger Hill, A Shau Valley,
Pleiku's gruesome streets and alleys,
Lam Son on Cambodia's trail,
Each a valiant, bloodstained tale.

Should they heed these lessons taught
Of why we served and why we fought.
Each place a part, a pledge forsaken,
To stay the fight, to peace awaken.

On march we soldiers, chosen men,
To fight the fights, again and again,
And though we know our fate's decreed,
You should know why we soldier's bleed.

For this our message, us to you,
We both have failed in what we do,
For we who fought, no victory won
Life can't be bettered with a gun,

And you who watch us on parade
With ticker tape as victories fade,
Must hear our voices, as we roar,
Both sides fighting lose each war,

These thoughts pop up at the strangest places, unbidden, undeniable, unheeded.

MEA CULPA
(Or Not)

As I lay me down to rest,
And put aside the day's last test,
Ten thousand nights and many more,
And still I dream about my war.

I want it just to go away,
To not be with me day to day,
And if I try with all my might,
I may not dream of war tonight.

Or shudder at a sound too loud,
Or feel so trapped in any crowd,
But still I do and try to hide,
The war which hovers at my side.

I've been to meetings, took the pills,
Talked to shrinks about my ills,
But just a whiff of gasoline,
Or rolling hills a bit too green,
A hint of gunfire's popping round,
A moan, a cry, a panicked sound,
And all those years come crashing down,
And I'm right back in Phu Bai town.

I don't stay long because I dread,
The memories still inside my head.
Yet when I leave I don't get far,
I only bear another scar.

You'd think by now the war would fade,
Replaced with sweet dreams I have made
Since coming home, civilian days,
Lots of Fords and Chevrolets.

Yet all those toys along the way,
Still roll aside when bugles play,
Or when I watch our flag's brave wave,
And think about how much we gave.

Right then it's not so long ago,
And what I need you most to know,
Ten thousand days and many more,
Can't cover up the pain we bore.

Our dead still sleep eternal sleep.
Our wounded's scars still run as deep,
And I'm still trying every day,
To push my Asian war away.

So every night before I sleep,
Or lay there counting khaki sheep,
I pray my war will fade away
And not be there at breaking day.

And then a **CLICK***, a rifle sound…*

My endless cycle, at least thus far, and not much further left to go.

571

Our unit patch, the badge I wore,
Binds us today as years before,
Strangers first, with little clue
Of what we were about to do.

A Dustoff Unit we were told,
"To Save A Life" our mission bold,
Common cause, embrace or go,
No 3rd choice, because we'd know,
Who was in, and who was out,
Had to know, no room for doubt.

Hot business this, we soon did learn,
As we, our combat wings did earn,
Flying in for brave men down,
Flying out our mission's crown.

We knew that doing what we did,
Took us most where danger hid,
Our ships would crash,
Our comrades die,
But on and on we chose to fly.

1000 men and even more,
We rescued, pulled from Death's grim door,
We flew each mission as we must,
A solemn vow, a sacred trust.

571, my unit name,
Scarce glory there and little fame,
But among ourselves we can relate,
I'll wear my patch at Glory's Gate.

Deep pride, deep appreciation, genuine bafflement at how I got through it all.

MERITORIOUS UNIT COMMENDATION.

By direction of the Secretary of the Army, under the provisions of paragraph 203, AR 672-5-1, the Meritorious Unit Commendation is awarded to the following named units of the United States Army for exceptionally meritorious achievement in the performance of outstanding service during the periods indicated. The citations read as follows:

1. THE 571ST MEDICAL DETACHMENT (HELICOPTER AMBULANCE)

The 571st MEDICAL DETACHMENT (HELICOPTER AMBULANCE) distinguished itself in support of Military Operations in the Republic of Vietnam during the period 1 September 1967 to 30 August 1968. Exhibiting untiring perseverance and profound dedication, the detachment provided rapid and comprehensive medical evacuation support to elements located throughout the Republic of Vietnam. During this period the unit went through activation, oversea deployment and an in-country move with exceptional efficiency in mission accomplishment. In February 1968, the organization was deployed to the Hue/Phu Bai area, thereby becoming the only helicopter ambulance detachment in the northern I Corps Tactical Zone. Despite the inherent hazards of enemy fire, rough terrain and inclement weather, the group recorded nearly four thousand missions and evacuated ten thousand sick and wounded patients with only six helicopters. As participants in the A Shau Valley, the 571st MEDICAL DETACHEMNT displayed exemplary courage and indomitable fortitude in providing excellent evacuation assistance during hostile fire situations. Through its singular initiative, excellent judgment and outstanding technical skill, the detachment contributed immeasurably to the free world effort against communist aggression in the Republic of Vietnam. The remarkable proficiency and devotion to duty displayed by the members of the 571st MEDICAL DETACHMENT are in keeping with the highest traditions of the military service and reflect distinct credit upon themselves and the Armed Forces of the United States.

EPITAPH

I flew Dustoff as a young man,
Didn't have to, volunteered.

Now, as old age replays my every miscue, trumpets every
blunder,
Remember that.

Weary as I am,
Apart from fame and fortune as I may be,

I flew Dustoff as a young man,
Didn't have to, volunteered.

Once we were your children.
Off to fight a war
Today we are your grandparents.
Hear us as we shout,
Beware!
Past is prelude.

Seated from Left: Pete Leonard, Don Avdul, Vince Cedola, John Chisolm, Jack Leininger, unknown
Standing, from Left: Jim Ziemba, Dick Long, Ken Hogan, Larry Woodyard, Bill Cook, Freddie Long, Gary Yeck, the Author, Bob Peneguy, Dave Comer, Willie Jackson

**Dustoff Reunion,
Las Vegas, Nevada
2014**

WHAT I LEARNED

War is hell.   *War is sublime.*   *War is degrading.*

War is uplifting.   *War breeds hatred.*

War enhances compassion War ruins lives. War builds character.

War exposes cowards.   *War ignores heroes.*

War is the poorest choice.   *War is necessary.*   *War is deadly.*

War is exhilarating.   *War seduces young men.*

Young men are easy to seduce.

No soldier leaves a war unwounded. All wounds are not visible.

Nobody wins a war. Victory is an illusion. Defeat is temporary.

Rationalization doesn't work. Neither does stereotyping. Denial is a temporary bandage.

Death is forever. Life is precious.

Amen.

GLOSSARY OF TERMS
(Of Endearment and Otherwise)

3rd Mar Div"	3rd Marine Division. Tough guys. Very.
"506"	Radio call sign for the Commanding Officers, 571st Dustoff.
"APC"	Armored Personnel Carrier. A tank without a cannon. Carried troops, usually to places they didn't want to go.
"Arc Light"	B-52 Bomber strikes. Lit up the sky, lit up the jungle.
"ARVN"	South Vietnamese soldier.
"A Shau Valley"	Bad bush. North Vietnamese stronghold.
"Baby- San"	Any Vietnamese child, male or female. Also any baby-faced, American.
"Bac-Si"	Medic, in Vietnamese.
"Bamboo Vipers"	Deadly, little snakes.
Bau-Me-Bau"	Vietnamese Budweiser. Yeah, it really had formaldehyde in it.
"Beaucoup ti-ti"	Very, very, short. Some kind of French/Vietnamese combo.
"Beehive Rounds"	Very nasty artillery shells packed with hundreds of small darts. Made to burst in the air, then kill everything in a very large area.
"Berm"	The perimeter of a base camp or firebase. Lots of barbed wire and dead foliage.
"Big Tet"	Tet Offensive 1968. Lots of fighting. Everywhere.
"Bloopers"	M-79 Grenade launcher.
"Boom-boom tricks"	Prostitutes. Boom-boom was slang for healthy

honeymoon activity.

"Boonie Hat"   Floppy, short brimmed cap, optional head gear, very chic.

"Bought the farm"   Died. Dead, once removed.

"Bringing Pee"   Streams of automatic weapons fire, also very nasty. Looked like flaming water from a hose.

"Butter bar LT"   A second lieutenant, usually very new in country, not always dangerous, but...

"Catching Z's"   Sleeping, napping.

"Cherry Boys"   Youngsters in uniform. Assumed to be virgins. Not for long.

"Chieu-hoi"   "I Surrender" in Vietnamese, allegedly.

"Cobras"   Two kinds, one a very nasty snake, big brother to Kraits and Vipers. The other, a two man super gunned up helicopter gunship.

"Concertina Wire"   Accordion spooled barbed wire, now very stylish in schoolyards.

"Death Card Aces"   Specially printed playing cards, usually the Ace of Spades, left on enemy bodies.

"DEROS"   Date Estimated Return from Overseas. Army talk for getout of Nam free date.

"Di-di Mau"   Get out, screw, go away, fast. Vietnamese (I think).

"Dinky-dau"   Crazy, loopy, more pidgin Vietnamese.

"DMZ"   Demilitarized Zone. A buffer area, No Man's Land.

"Donut Dollies"   Red Cross volunteer workers (female).

"ETA"   Estimated Time of Arrival"

"Flying Cav" — Helicopter borne sky soldiers.

"Free Fire Zones" — Places not to go. Anything out there, shoot it.

"Getting short" — Getting close to your going home day (see DEROS).

"Hooches" — Tropical barracks.

"Humping Ruck" — Traipsing through the jungle, carrying lots of stuff. Very difficult.

"Jody" — This is the guy our drill instructors told us (guaranteed us actually) would be stealing our girlfriends and wives while we were away. Not quite sure why they had to be so definite about this, but they were.

"Jungle feet" — Foot diseases, fungus that doesn't go away.

"K-bar knives" — Marine Corps issue bayonet. Handy.

"Kraits" — Some type of crazy relative of the bamboo viper. Also deadly.

"LBJ" — Lyndon Baines Johnson, 36th President of the United States, did not lose the war. (He said so).

"Loaches" — Small, two man helicopters used for observation and attracting enemy fire.

"Mama-sans" — Female papa-sans.

"Multiple frags" — Lots of fragmentation wounds, usually from mortar rounds. Nasty.

"Ninety One Bravo" — (91B) Military Occupational Designation for a Medic.

"Nomex Suits" — Flameproof flight uniforms, we hoped.

"Numbah One" — The best, a good guy, usually marked by generosity.

"Numbah Ten" — The worst, a bad guy, usually a cheapskate.

"Papa-sans"   *Any male Vietnamese who was not a baby-san.*

"Plasma Hotel"   *Radio call sign for the 85th Evac Hospital.*

"Poncho Liners"   *Lightweight blanket thing, waterproof, a good thing.*

"Poppin' smoke"   *Signaling with a smoke grenade.*

"Puff or Smoky"   *Fixed wing gunships. Lotsa bullets.*

"Punji Stakes"   *Sharpened bamboo stakes, buried point up in the ground, not very deep. A VC booby trap meant to infect and kill.*

"REMF's"   *Rear Echelon Mother-(you know, the f-word).*

"ROK's"   *Republic of Korea soldiers. Bad mother-you knows.*

"Rolling Thunder"   *B-52 bomber strikes. Very Apocalypse Now.*

"RPG"   *Rocket propelled grenade. Shoulder fired bazooka thing.*

"RTO's"   *Radio-Telephone Operators.*

"Skids light"   *Helicopter aloft.*

"Sucking Chests"   *Very serious chest wounds, usually involving a punctured lung.*

"Tac Push"   *Tactical Frequency, radio band used for medevacs which left our primary frequency available for more missions.*

"T&T's"   *Through and through gunshot wounds. In one side, out the other.*

"Willie Pete"   *White Phosphorous. Artillery delivered napalm-like nasty stuff.*

"Xin Loi"   *I'm sorry, in Vietnamese, I guess.*

If you enjoyed this book, please take a few moments to write a review on your favorite store, and refer it to your friends. Share your views, how else will anyone know?

Lightning Source UK Ltd.
Milton Keynes UK
UKHW020755240223
417576UK00009B/92

9 781513 668031